With Lord Byron
— at the —
Sandwich Islands
— in 1825 —

Being Extracts from the MS Diary of James Macrae, Scottish Botanist.

— HONOLULU —

— 1922 —

List of Illustrations

❖❖❖

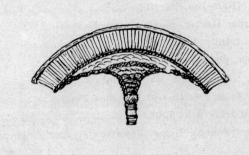

Foreword

KING LIHOLIHO IOLANI (Kamehameha II.) and his queen, Kamamalu, died in London while on a visit to see their "great and good friend" George IV. In order to show its respect for the royal pair who had travelled so far and who had come to such an untimely end, the British government sent their remains back to Honolulu in the Blonde frigate, commanded by George Anson, seventh Lord Byron, who happened to be first cousin to the poet and successor to his title, and who was also a grandson of Admiral Byron of the Dolphin, one of the British explorers in the Pacific previous to Captain Cook.

The Horticultural Society of London (now the Royal Horticultural Society), hearing of the intended departure of the Blonde for the Sandwich Islands, and wishing to help the natives of that group, obtained permission to send on the Blonde a fine collection of plants, considered suitable for the climate of "Owhyee" under the charge of James Macrae, a young Scotsman, trained as a plant collector and horticulturist. The plants were to be distributed as a gift among the chiefs of the islands. By the same opportunity, John Wilkinson, a skilled agriculturist, was induced, evidently through promises held out to him by Boki, one of the chiefs who had come to London in the train of the deceased King Liholiho, to come out to Honolulu with the intention of starting some kind of tropical farm on land to be given him by Boki.

Hitherto, the only published account of the voyage of the Blonde is the work compiled by Mrs. Maria Graham, and issued in London in 1826. This work is supposed to have been based on materials supplied by the diary kept by Mr. Bloxom, the chaplain to the Blonde, supplemented by details taken from the diary or journal of one of the midshipmen on board the same vessel. The writer of "An Examination of Charges against the American Missionaries at the Sandwich Islands as alleged in the Voyage of the ship Blonde and in the London Quarterly Review," published at Cambridge (U.S.A.) 1827, has a very poor opinion of this account of the voyage as set forth by Mrs. Graham, and terms it "nearly worthless."

During the course of the voyage of the Blonde to and from the Sandwich Islands, which included visits to various ports en route, James Macrae, when he had the chance, was a diligent collector of plants and objects of natural history. On returning to England in 1826, his herbarium and diary were handed over to his patron the Horticultural Society. The herbarium was probably delivered to Kew or the British Museum in order that the various plants collected by Macrae might be scientifically catalogued and described. His manuscript diary, however, has reposed, until this date, on the shelves of the library of the Royal Horticultural Society. The present writer thought it would be worth while to have that portion of Macrae's journal which refers to the Sandwich or Hawaiian group made known to the public. He has therefore obtained the consent of the Council of the Royal Horticultural Society to its being published.

To those who are interested in the early history of the Sandwich, or as they are now termed, the Hawaiian Islands, it is believed that in Macrae's Journal will be found some curious glimpses of men and manners as they existed in the islands at the close of the first quarter of the nineteenth century. The Hawaiian chiefs and people were then beginning to come in contact with the haole or white man, but were still masters in their own land. The people grew their own taro and caught their own fish, and did not rely on Asiatics to do it for them. They were still living in grass houses built by themselves and they were clad in the native tapa or kapa cloth.

Like his fellow countrymen, Doctor Archibald Menzies and David Douglas, who had visited and explored the Hawaiian Islands, James Macrae was a botanist and mountain climber, and the account of his visits to Mauna Kea and Kilauea Volcano and his rambles on the island of Oahu are worth preserving.

After his return to England, Macrae was appointed by the British Colonial office to the post of superintendent of what was then called the Colonial Gardens at Ceylon. Whether or not these gardens were at Colombo or at what is now called the Royal Botanic Gardens at Peradenyia, near Kandy, the present writer has, so far, been unable to find out. Neither has he been able to ascertain anything further about the career of Macrae. As Macrae was a collector and outdoor man, botanical writers have little to say about Macrae. Had he been a "systematist," a party such as Linnaeus or de Candolle, who sat at home at ease and catalogued the plants that had been gathered by hardy explorers like Macrae, then no doubt we would have known more about the facts of his life.

In the botanical world Macrae is remembered by *Macraea,* a tribe of Chilian plants belonging to the order of *Geraniaceae,* and in the Hawaiian flora, several plants have Macrae for their trivial names.   Some of these may be mentioned here, viz.:

		Native Name.
Asplenium Macraei	Hook. & Grev.	Pamoho
Coreopsis Macraei	Gray	
Cyathodes Macraei	D. C.	Maieli or Puakeawe
Cyrtandra Macraei	Gray	
Davallia Macraeana	Hook. & Arn.	Laukahi
Depavia Macraei	Hook. & Grev.	
Peperomia Macraeana	D. C.	Alaala wainui
Phyllostegia Macraei	Bentham	Kapana
Rubus Macraei	Gray	Akala
Vaccinium Macraenum	Klotzsch	Ohelo

In the Index Kewensis Plantarum, other plants named after Macrae may be found.

Mrs. Maria Graham, the compiler of "The Voyage of the Blonde," does not mention Macrae by name, but the following sentences in her work refer to him.   "It is to be regretted that the practised collector of botanical specimens who went in the Blonde to the Sandwich Islands, should not have furnished any account of the plants, useful and curious, which he collected for the Horticultural Society, or that some of the very enlightened members of that society should not have done so. The field is in some respects new; and it is acknowledged by all the foreign navigators that the collection made during the Blonde's voyage is one of the most curious in Europe."

The undersigned has added a condensed Log of the Blonde before reaching and after leaving the Sandwich Islands. He has also appended explanatory notes to Macrae's Diary, and furnished several illustrations taken from engravings, photographs and autographs in his private collection.

WM. F. WILSON.

Honolulu, September 30, 1922.

NOTES ON VOYAGE H.M.S. BLONDE FROM WOOLWICH, LONDON, TO HILO, HAWAII

1824

Sept. 8—H.M.S. Blonde of 46 guns, commanded by Captain Lord Byron, then lying at Woolwich, received on board the bodies of the late King and Queen of the Sandwich Islands.

     " 28—The suite of Sandwich Islanders got on board at Spithead, and the ship sailed the same day.

Oct. 18—Reached Madeira and stayed there until 23rd Oct.

Nov. 27—Reached Rio de Janeiro and left on Dec. 18 for St. Catherines for the purpose of obtaining provisions and water.

Dec. 24—Reached St. Catherines and sailed again on Jan. 1, 1825

Feby. 4—Anchored in Valparaiso Bay .

     " 8—Kapihe, "Admiral of the Sandwich Islands," and one of the late King's suite, died today from an attack of apoplexy. He was a skilled player at the Hawaiian game of draughts, called "konane."

Mar. 16—Reached Callao.

     " 25—Arrived at Galapagos Islands, and stayed there until April 2.

April 3—Boki, who had already been baptized at the islands, partook of the Lord's Supper.

May 1—Liliha and the other Sandwich Islanders on board were baptized by the chaplain of the Blonde. Lord Byron was their sponsor.

     " 3—Land sighted off the coast of Hilo, Island of Hawaii.

IOLANI
(King Kamehameha II.)

From a life sketch made in London

James Macrae's Diary

H.M.S. "BLONDE" ARRIVES AT HILO, HAWAII

May 3, 1825.   Made the S.E. point of Owhyee, and at 12
got close in with the land, which afforded us a pleasant contrast
to the Galapagos Islands lately left.   Here green slopes were seen
beautifully interspersed with trees, and in many places along the
coast, rows of coco-nuts with leaning bushy tops.   The country
in this part rose inland with a gentle ascent, and did not appear
to us much intersected by deep ravines.

By 2 o'clock p.m. we hove too off Heddo Bay, and lowered
two of the ship's boats, one for the surveyor and his assistant,
and the other for the master to go in shore to try soundings in
order to ascertain whether we could return here to refit the vessel
after depositing the bodies of the King and Queen of the Sandwich Islands at the seat of government at Woahoo.   While the
boats were away two ragged white men came on board and reported that the ship was standing on not far from a reef which lay
most way across the mouth of the bay.   All was instantly bustle
and noise to put the ship about and stand out to sea farther from
the land.

We learned from these men that news had been brought them
a month ago, by an English whaler from the port of London, of
the King and Queen's[1] death.   We were also informed that the

---

[1]Liholiho and Kamamalu.   The name Liholiho or Rihoriho is a
contraction of Kalaninuiliholiho (the great black (?) heaven).   On
state occasions, Liholiho was induced to take the title of Kamehameha
II., but his favorite name was Iolani (the great Io or god of heaven).
Io was the supreme deity of Polynesia, and "his name was held to
be so sacred that none but the priest might utter it at certain times
and places" (Tregear).   Io was recognized in New Zealand and at
Tahiti and other islands in the South Seas.   In Hindustan, the home
of the Polynesian race, Io is known as Deo, Dyu or Dyo.   In the ceremony of fire-walking or "umuti" as practised at Raiatea Island, the
priest, before leading his followers across the fiery pit, invoked the
aid of the supreme god Io.   Although the word Io appears in Andrews'
Hawaiian dictionary under eleven different headings, none of these
mention that one meaning for the word is that of the great deity of
Polynesia.   Liholiho having been initiated into the inner mysteries of
the Hawaiian temple, must have understood the signification of the
word, and hence his fondness for it as one of his own names.   The
inscription in poor Hawaiian, on the outer coffin made in England for
the body of Liholiho, winds up as follows: "Aloka ino no komakoa
Elii Jiolani," i.e., "Aloha ino no ko makou Alii Iolani," or in English,
"Deep love to our chief Iolani."
Kamamalu is a contraction of Kamehamehamalu (the shade of

natives of the island of Atooi to leeward, had rebelled two months
ago against the Regent in consequence of the chief of that island
having died since the king went to England, and that owing to
the arrival from America some months past of the son and heir to
the deceased chief, who claimed the rights of his father. Before
he was defeated by the superior force of the Regent, who commanded in person, the rebellion occasioned the loss of upwards of
two thousand natives, besides two Europeans. Yet we were assured that this same chief, after being captured, is at present suffered to go at large in the town of Hanarura at Woahoo.

We had not been long off the bay of Heddo when several of
the natives visited us from the shore, paddling off in their canoes,
and bringing with them sugar canes, taro (*arum spec.*), fish and
hogs. The sugar canes were generally of the purple and striped
kind and of a large size. The dress of the men consisted of the
maro, a piece of various dyed cloth of their own manufacture,
eight or ten inches broad, and about three yards long, which they
pass between the legs and tie around the waist. The dress of the
women consisted generally of a larger piece of cloth of similar
manufacture, tied carelessly around the waist, forming a short
petticoat reaching halfway down the thigh. This was the common dress of all who came off to the ship, excepting that of the
head chief, who is commonly honored with the title of governor,
and that of one of his wives. Both were of more than ordinary
size from overgrown corpulency. The governor's dress consisted
of a dirty cotton shirt, a pair of blue China nankeen trousers and
an old straw hat. That of his wife, the common petticoat used
by the other females, with the addition of a piece of native made
cloth tied round her neck, hanging loosely over her body and open
in front like a cloak. Both these, on coming on board, touched
noses, after the manner of salutation of their country, with most
of the Sandwich Islanders we had brought out from England, and
immediately after went with them below to their cabins, where
they all soon commenced a disagreeable howling noise in lamenta-
tion of their late king and queen.

All the canoes of the natives that came alongside the ship
had outriggers, the same as described by Capt. Cook and others.
That in which the governor came on board was upwards of 40
feet long and very neatly made.

Kamehameha), contracted to Kamehamalu and afterwards to Kamamalu. On the brass plate fixed to the coffin made for her in England,
she is termed "Tamehamalu Eli," i.e., "Kamehamalu Alii."

At five o'clock the boats returned, bringing information that the anchorage was good and the entrance to it sufficiently large for ships of the line.

SAILS FOR MAUI

We now made sail for the island of Mowee, where, his Lordship was informed, Queen Kanamanah[2] at present resided, to take her on board with any other people of consequence on that island who might wish to be present at the funeral, like the governor and his wife, who, with several others, had already come on board at Heddo. The neighborhood of Heddo Bay to the east, is thickly covered with wood from the seacoast everywhere back in the interior as far as we could see. The country is free from fog, and to the west much intersected with deep ravines ending by the sea in abrupt cliffs, down which fall several beautiful cascades of water.

The native huts appeared most numerous round the edge of the bay, being pleasantly situated under thick groves of coco-nut and bread fruit trees. Among the numerous trees that ornament this delightful spot, are numbers of the candlenut (*aleurites*) so easily distinguished at a long distance by their white shining leaves. These grow everywhere on the coast.

May 4. Saw the summit of Mouna Kaah[3] towering far above the clouds, and in places covered with snow. We also saw Mauna Roa appearing not far off from the other, but without snow. The grand appearance of both these mountains as seen from on board the ship, upwards of 100 miles out at sea, would repay the traveller for coming so far on purpose to see them.

We had scarcely done looking at the mountains of Owhyee, when the highland of Mowee appeared in a similar way ahead, but nowhere covered with snow.

WEST MAUI

In the course of the next hour or two, we were running along the shore under the high land, and we noticed that this side of the island was intersected with numerous deep ravines, down which fell several waterfalls, at no great distance from each other. These were admired by all on board, most of whom anxiously desired to be on shore that they might satisfy their thirst

2Kaahumanu.
3Mauna Kea .

from such beautiful water. For the last month we had been on short allowance of this article, which was often served out not drinkable. The land on this side of Mowee rose to the peaks of the mountains much more steeply than anywhere noticed at Owyhee. Like that island it was well wooded, and along the coast covered with verdure, yet little cultivated, although the native huts appeared everywhere more numerous and at no great distance from each other, generally upon the ridges near the coast for the convenience of fishing.

LAHAINA

When we got near enough to the shore we lowered a boat and landed all the Sandwich Island people brought from England. These were dressed in new mourning suits, which formed a rare contrast beside their naked countrymen. When they landed on the beach, they were received by some thousands of natives making a very disagreeable loud howling noise, ceasing at intervals for a few minutes, then commencing again as before, which they kept up in this manner most of the night. About seven, came to anchor in eleven fathoms on a coral bottom, not far from a reef with a high surf on it. During the night a native schooner was sent to Woahoo to inform Mr. Pitt[4] and Mr. Charlton[5] of our arrival.

May 5. A fine morning. Lowered the ship's boats for the purpose of getting a fresh supply of water. Got permission to go ashore, but promised not to go out of sight of the ship, it being uncertain when we might get under weigh. On going ashore I met three poor ragged white men at the watering place, who offered their services to accompany me through the native huts and plantations. To a stranger it was difficult to find the nearest way, from the numerous taro ponds almost everywhere among the huts. The taro, I noticed, was cultivated to a greater extent than any other esculent. The ponds of water in which they cultivated it, are commonly square and of different sizes, about four feet deep from the level surface, and the bottom covered with

[4]William or Billy Pitt, the nickname given by foreigners to Kalanimoku or Kalaimoku, governor of the island of Oahu.

[5]Richard Charlton, first British consul to the Sandwich Islands. His jurisdiction as consul extended to the Society and Friendly Islands. Died at Falmouth, England, on 25th December, 1852.

water to a depth of from 2 to 2½ feet. The water is constantly supplied from a neighboring stream by means of a small canal emptying itself from one pond to another, until at last it reaches the seashore. These ponds are used for keeping fish and ducks as well as for growing taro. In general they are kept free from weeds and rushes, and are planted with surprising regularity, not far behind what one would expect from a more civilized race of people. The singular method which they have adopted of growing this farinaceous esculent always in water has originated beyond doubt at an early period with themselves. Perhaps it was from their extreme fondness for that element which they so often frequent during the day, in a manner similar to the feathered aquatic tribe. When they have occasion to weed these ponds, they are generally up in mud and water above the knees, which to any other race not so much accustomed to water, would be found inconvenient. They, as far as I could learn, have no particular season for planting or for taking up the taro, but go on using the largest roots as they occasionally want them for food from the ponds that are most forward till they become nearly done. Then they turn the water off and drain the pond dry, placing whatever fish it may contain into the nearest pond. The old ponds from which the taro has been harvested are left for a few days exposed to the sun for the mud to harden. Then round or square clumps are thrown up about two feet high and seven or eight in circumference, at short distances from each other, always in straight lines, either across or lengthwise. In these clumps are planted the crowns of the taro, from eight to twelve in number alternately about a foot apart. The crowns which they choose for planting are the top parts of the taro cut across about half an inch, adhering to the leaves, which they shorten to the length of eight or nine inches.

Round the sides of the ponds, by the edge of the water, is often planted what they term the tea tree[6] (*dracaena terminalis*), the root of which they cook underground as is customary with them in everything else that requires cooking before it is eaten. This they afterwards pound and put into vessels full of water and let it remain there for a few days to ferment, when it makes a good substitute for beer of a very intoxicating quality. A piece of the cooked root which was brought to me to taste was as sweet

[6] In Hawaiian "Ti or "Ki."

as sugar cane, and in my opinion contained an equal quantity of saccharine matter. If the common process generally used for the making of sugar was here once to be introduced, it might be turned to the same advantage as sugar cane for manufacturing sugar. But whilst there is no emulation among the natives for commerce or cultivating more than is necessary to supply their present wants, the value that might likely be found out from this plant with so little trouble will probably yet remain for a length of time imperfectly known.

One of the said white men took me to his little garden which surrounded his hut. Here I noticed *Cytisus cajan* or the common pigeon pea of the West Indies, which he said was given him last year by the captain of an American whaler for coffee, together with some seeds of the lima bean (*Phaseolus lunatus*), both of which were now in bearing for some time. But being as yet unacquainted with the way of using them for food, he always felt afraid to touch them for that purpose. These, with a few light-red coloured cabbages, two sorts of sweet potatoes (the red and white), water melons, pumpkins, a few patches of sugar cane, two or three ponds of taro and some bitter gourds that are used by the natives for various purposes, such as calabashes, were, with a hog and a few fowls, all that he had for the support of himself and family.

His wife is a native woman, by whom he has had three children. He has often applied, without success, to the missionaries to baptize his children, but they are considered by them to be born out of wedlock.

Beyond the huts and plantations, I observed but few plants. Some were Cleome, Argemone, and two sorts of Malvas, three of Sidas[7] (two of which the natives use for wreaths and necklaces, by stringing the flowers on a thread made from the bark of the tapa plant). In the cultivated grounds of the natives I noticed they had no plantains and only three sorts of bananas. One of these was much shorter than the others, and different to any I had ever seen before. The red banana[8] common in Otahiti, has not

[7]The ilima of Hawaiians, until recent years very much used by them in making wreaths ("leis") for the head or neck. Ilima blossoms have given place to meaningless colored paper wreaths.

[8]Fei (musa fei or musa uranascopus) the wild mountain banana of Tahiti, which forms a considerable part of the daily menu of the natives of that island. The large bunch of fruit grows upright from

yet reached the Sandwich Islands, but will now, no doubt, soon be introduced by Mr. Charlton, who is to visit that Island once every year.

DESCRIPTION OF LAHAINA IN 1825.

The town of Lahaina on Mowee Island, is composed of a number of low thatched huts, scattered along the sea shore for about a mile in length, and in places nearly half that distance in breadth. It lies on a level flat at the foot of the high mountains which rise abruptly in the central part of the island. At the west end of the town is a small grove of coco-nut trees. More towards the town on the sea beach, is a mud battery in bad repair, mounted with five small cannon, in the same neglected state. Within its walls is a small mud hut, whitewashed outside, where had been buried lately one of Tamahamaah's queens.[9] Near this fort, the missionaries have a small thatched chapel, with dwelling houses and garden grounds. Here I was shown the only grape vine on the island. It was yet but young and never produced fruit.[10] Close to the beach, nearly in front of the town, stands a brick house of two low stories, whitewashed outside, built sixteen years ago by Tamahamaah for his favorite queen Kaumanna, which she never inhabited, choosing rather to live, after the native fashion, in a thatched hut close beside the other.

The town has no regular streets, being all cultivated and rather difficult to get from one end to the other on account of the taro ponds. It looked like a well cultivated garden, divided into allotments by mud walls enclosing each family hut and garden. Sugar canes grow with little trouble on the narrow ridges between the taro ponds, where they have also at times, cotton, tobacco,

the top of the stem instead of hanging down like the ordinary kind of banana. It requires to be cooked before being eaten. In Hillebrand's Flora, page 434, it is stated that the fei had been introduced into Oahu from Tahiti, and that it grows in a few of the higher ravines of Oahu. Is this a fact? Seemann states that this species of banana occurs in Fiji.

[9]Keopuolani, the bluest-blooded wife of Kamehameha I. She was mother of Liholiho (Kamehameha II.) and Kauikeaouli (Kamehameha III).

[10]After the date of Macrae's visit, Lahaina became celebrated for its grapes, and whenever an inter-island schooner or steamer touched there, shore boats came off laden with grapes, mangos, etc., for sale. This custom exists no longer.

and cabbages. The tapa tree (*Brousonettia*), from the bark of which they manufacture the cloth they wear, occupies a large proportion of their ground. It is neatly planted out in rows and kept free from weeds.

I was informed that the number of natives living at Lahaina exceeded 6000, and some years before had been far above that number, but since then hundreds had died in a short time from some unknown fever.

At four p.m. the ship's boats having brought off the necessary water and provisions, all on shore were ordered to return on board at once. At six we weighed anchor and made sail for the island of Woahoo, having on board about forty natives, among whom were the mother of the deceased queen, and her daughter, an interesting young girl of ten,[11] sister to the present youth proclaimed king. This princess was dressed in deep mourning brought her from England by Madame Boki. Several of the chiefs who came on board were also clothed in European fashion, while others of inferior rank had only a shirt and maro without a hat.

ARRIVES AT HONOLULU

May 6. Fine morning. Made the island of Woahoo and at 7 a.m. got under Diamond Head and saw the Bay of Wytitte covered with thick groves of coco-nut trees, where lay underneath many of the native huts. Behind these appeared the woody mountains rising in places abruptly and intersected by numerous valleys having on each side high peaked ridges covered with green forests.

At 8 we were off the harbor of Hanarura and made signal for the pilot. Shortly after, Captain Charlton came on board to conduct us to safe anchorage outside a coral reef which runs across the mouth of the harbour, nearly a mile from shore, and having only in one part opposite the town a narrow passage over a bar from 3 to 4 fathoms of water. This was thought too shallow for our ship going over to a more convenient place in the inner harbour. At 10 on coming to anchor in 20 fathoms we fired a salute of 15 guns, which was, to our surprise, returned with the same number from both forts on shore, where we noticed was

[11]Nahienaena.

NAHIENAENA
(Sister of Kamehameha III.)
At the age of 10

From painting by R. Dampier,
Artist of H.M.S. "Blonde."

hoisted the national flag,[12] having the Union of Britain in the upper corner.

In the harbour were three American merchant ships and several smaller vessels, two of which were native brigs mounted with 8 to 10 small guns. To the west of the harbour lay the wreck of a whale ship of 400 tons, from the port of London, wrecked two weeks ago during the night whilst waiting for the captain, who was on shore enjoying himself too freely. The crew saved themselves and her cargo of nearly 800 barrels of sperm oil, as also most of her spars, rigging, etc., have since been nearly all saved.

No one was allowed to go on shore today but the natives and his Lordship and the chaplain, who upon landing were met by crowds of the natives making the same howling noise as before when we were at the island of Mowee.

POI AND RAW FISH

Since we reached the islands, we have been much amused at the natives' simple manners, going to different parts of the ship, eagerly examining what they saw. At other times we were not a little disgusted when they sat down to their meals, eating raw fish with the gills and entrails and their fingers covered with blood. They appear to have no stated time for their meals, but ate when they felt inclined, sometimes as late as 12 o'clock at night, at other times by daylight in the morning. Their diet consisted of raw and dried fish and taro. The latter they generally pound with a mixture of cold water, on a thick board, with a stone, to nearly the same consistency as we do starch for linen.

[12]It is generally believed that the Hawaiian national flag was designed by a Scotsman, Captain Alexander Adams, who arrived at the islands in 1809, and resided there until his death in Honolulu on October 27th, 1871, at the advanced age of 91 years. He lies buried in Nuuanu Cemetery alongside his old crony, Andrew Auld. The inscription on their common tombstone reads as follows:

Sacred to the memory of

Alexander Adams,	Andrew Auld,
a native of	a native of
Arbroth (sic), Forfarshire,	Linlithgow, Scotland.
Scotland.	Born Sept. 8, 1799.
Born Dec. 27, 1780.	Died Oct. 26, 1873
Died Oct. 17, 1871	

"Twa croanies (sic) frae the land of heather,
Are sleepin' here in death th'gether."

Then it is put into calabashes till it is wanted to be eaten. This they term poi, and is, when they can procure fish to eat with it, their constant and favorite food. When a family has its meals they sit on the ground in a circle, with their calabashes of poi in the centre. In turns they keep dipping the right hand forefinger, somewhat bent, into the same dish, and then thrust the finger into their mouths. The poi tasted to me sour and unpalatable, but when sweetened with sugar was greatly improved, and some on board liked it.

NATIVE MODE OF MEASUREMENT

The unusual size of our ship greatly attracted the natives, and when they came on board they began to fathom her length from stern to bow along the bulwark, at other times laying themselves flat on the quarter deck. Their knowledge of measurement appeared to us to be very imperfect, only amounting to a calculation of fathoms taken by the hands, dependent on memory. This is different from the Africans, who tally their numbers by notches on a stick.

At 8 o'clock p.m. we were again surprised to hear the gun from the fort, as is customary at that hour with the garrisons of other nations.

KAUIKEAOULI, NAHIENAENA AND KALANIMOKU

May 7. Went on shore with Lord Byron and most of the principal officers. On landing we were met by Capt. Charlton and a number of the chiefs ready to join us in a procession to Mr. Pitt (Kramaku's)[13] house for the purpose of being introduced. The chiefs were all dressed in European costume, and on our leaving the landing place, they in friendly manner placed one of us between every two of themselves, each having hold of our arm, till we reached Pitt's house, a small thatched hut pleasantly situated near the farther end of the town, within a large garden fenced in with high poles standing upright.

Pitt was dressed in black. His visage is thin and he is defective of an eye, but is by no means unpleasant in his manners. At the upper end of the hut was a platform raised about a foot from the floor, covered with the same kind of mats as the

[13]Kalaimoku or Kalanimoku, alias Billy Pitt.

KAUIKEAOULI
(Kamehameha III.), at the age of 11

From painting by R. Dampier,
Artist of H.M.S. "Blonde."

rest of the hut. Here the young king[14] and his sister[15], whom we had brought from Mowee, were seated on a shabby sofa placed crossways, and having at the backs of it several handsome large feather plumes of various colours, customarily used by them in former times when at war and on high festivals.

Both looked delicate and of rather dark complexion. They had full nostrils and large mouths, but had fine open countenances, with good eyes and teeth, and not altogether wanting a sensibility of look that rendered them engaging. The king wore a short blue jacket with shirt and pantaloons, without shoes or stockings. His sister was in the said mourning dress from England.

From the king's sofa on the right, the principal chiefs and general officers stood in a line alongside the hut. From his sister on the left, lay on the mats by her sofa, Queen Kaumanna and two more of their father's[16] wives still living. After these three, stood, according to their seniority, five of their deceased brother's[17] wives, joined by a number of other female chiefesses, to the bottom of the hut. These were dressed in black canton crepe or silk of the same colour, with shoes and silk stockings and showy combs in their hair, everyway neatly dressed, contrary to what we all expected to find these people. When the ceremony of being introduced to the Regent (Billy Pitt) was over, through the Spaniard (Mr. Marin[18]) who acted as interpreter, the presents brought from England were then presented to His Majesty by Lord Byron.

PRESENTS FROM ENGLAND

The presents were a suit of full dress Windsor uniform, an elegant sword and a gold watch, with the arms of the king of Great Britain engraved on the back. Pitt was presented with a handsome gold ring. The king immediately tried on his clothes, and found it fitted as if made for him. He looked extremely well in them and was proud when he had on his cocked

[14]Kauikeaouli (Kamehameha III).

[15]Nahienaena.

[16]Widows of Kamehameha I.

[17]Widows of Kamehameha II.

[18]Francisco de Paula Marin, known to the Hawaiians as Manini. He is said to have had 52 children, thus carrying into effect King Kalakaua's motto "Hooulu lahui," "Increase the nation." Marin died 30th Oct., 1837, aged 64 years. Came to the islands about 1794.

hat and sword, walking about speaking to some of his subjects.

When the presentation ceremony was over we were ordered to sit on chairs arranged for us in the middle of the hut. Country wine, made the year before, was offered to us by Mr. Marin. Some sat tasting the wine, and others got introduced to the females who were now sitting on mats. They could only answer with a smile, not knowing our language. The queens were all of enormous bulk, and by no means handsome.

THE HORTICULTURAL SOCIETY OF LONDON

Being tired of waiting any longer at this mock formality, I slipped away unperceived, to look for plants, but being missed by Lord Byron, I was sent for to return, and was presented to the Regent as the person who had brought them plants from the Horticultural Society of London. He was informed that I wanted permission to collect the wild plants of the country for the Society. Mr. Pitt, Regent, kindly granted me full liberty to collect what plants I wished. Lord Byron, however, requested me not to begin collecting until the funeral was over.

HONOLULU IN 1825

In the afternoon, with some of the officers, I went for a walk through the town, which is situated on a sandy flat, with scarcely a tree for shade, except a few coco-nut trees in groups in places along the beach. The native huts are small and thatched with grass from top to bottom, but there are others inhabited by some Europeans and chiefs, which are covered over with mud, half a yard thick, to prevent accidents by fire, which so often occur in the others. These are better finished inside, and the floors spread over with mats made from rushes or the leaves of pandanus.

The huts of the poorer classes are mere hovels, having a low door placed where they creep on hands and knees to get out and in, with nothing to cover the opening hut a piece of cloth or mat. Some of these into which we looked out of curiosity, had a hog or two tied up in a corner, and in others a dog nearly hairless from mange. The stench from having these animals live with them in the same hut was most offensive. There are as yet only four or five houses built after the European manner. One belongs to an American merchant, another to Mr. Pitt, not yet finished, part of

HONOLULU

(Looking towards the Fort and Alewa Heights.)

Drawn by L. Choris.

which is at present converted into a guard house for a few naked soldiers who do duty at times by way of mounting guard in front of the king's hut, after a peculiar fashion of their own.

They do this in the following manner. Six or eight of these turn out together and form a line (not a straight one), and keep walking backwards and forwards, one after another, till they are dismissed. While they are in this way on duty, he that is last or foremost rings a small bell which is carried in the hand by way of signal for the others to turn either backwards or forwards. Their accoutrements are not all alike. Some have only a bayonet in their hand, held upright or reversed, just as suits their convenience, while another has an old rusty long barreled musket of American make, without a flint and sometimes a lock. Some have a cartouche box tied on behind with a piece of untanned goat skin, others have it in front and some have none at all.

The town of Hanarura contains about five or six hundred houses, and if the number of its inhabitants is taken at about ten to a hut, where they generally live together in families of two or three generations, they will amount to about 6000, which, I think, is underrated. Their huts are built without any regular form, enclosed with low mud walls, and a small garden, but without taro ponds the same as we saw at Mowee. Some of these gardens are cultivated with tobacco, Indian corn, water melons, pumpkins, etc., while others suffer weeds to grow and neglect cultivation, preferring to use them as a stockyard for hogs, goats, dogs and poultry.

THE HARBOUR AND PUNCHBOWL FORTS

Beside the harbour they have built a fort of mud and coral rock picked up at low tide. It is square and mounted with upward of 50 guns, many of which are 18 pounders, got from the Americans in exchange for sanders wood. From its situation it is not capable of long defense from an enemy at sea off the mouth of the harbour. It is at present in bad repair, and is in charge of an old Irishman, who has been on the island for many years.

About a mile above the town on the top of a hill[19] with the appearance of a volcano, they have another fort that mounts ten

[19]Puowaina or Punchbowl Hill.

guns, which command the town and the taro ponds with other provisions cultivated in a large valley well watered by two rivers which run on each side till they meet in one behind the town.

Among the many Americans who live on the island, two keep public houses for the accommodation of strangers where they have managed to introduce a billiard table each, and are supplied with all kinds of spirits as well as wine at times from their country whale ships touching here for fresh provisions and water.

SEES THE HULA

May 8. Sunday. Went on shore after dinner with several of the gentlemen from on board. Met Mr. Charlton, who agreed upon tomorrow for me to go with him to Mr. Pitt to arrange matters about my going to the woods collecting. Mr. Charlton offered me the use of three of his jackasses brought from England, to carry myself and specimens. These, I assured him, would be more hindrance than use, and asked him for three natives in preference, but in the end I was obliged to accept one jackass, as he would take no denial. He promised to have ready what natives I wanted as well as a guide.

In the cultivated grounds above the town, I noticed some good sugar canes, mostly of the purple striped kind, and a few patches of potatoes with weak stems not likely to be productive. Returned on board in the evening having been much amused observing the natives' simple manners and mode of dancing, which they accompany with a song and graceful motions of the arms and body, raising their voice at intervals to a high key, then again lowering it, without any given certain time that had in the least resemblance to music.

The inhabitants here all approached us without the least timidity like those we saw at the other islands, probably arising from greater intercourse with foreigners. Several could speak a good many words of English, to whom they are much attached, and often we heard the word "Britanee maitee," which means "English very good" and superior to people of other nations, whom they look upon with jealousy.

SANDAL WOOD TRADE

May 9.[19]a. Got nothing arranged as promised by Mr. Charlton as to my collecting, owing to the preparations making for the
funeral. The natives load vessels annually with sanders[20] wood
for which they get in exchange European and Chinese manufac-
tured goods with every advantage to the foreigners. So eager, I
was informed, have the traders been since the discovery of this
native wood by one of themselves, named Brown,[21] in 1810, that
every kind of scheme has been entered into for supplying the government with such articles as they thought would most attract
notice and likely to be purchased. For this purpose they have
introduced slight vessels built of fir, fitted with showy cabins with
looking glasses, sofas with red morocco cushions, etc., and sold
them at the enormous price of 80,000 dollars[22] to be paid for in
sanders wood as it could be got from the different islands, without
further trouble to themselves than the bringing it to the sea beach.
For the traders themselves have small craft constantly in the harbour of Hanarura where they have on shore large store houses for
the convenience of lading vessels. Besides vessels, the traders
have furnished the natives with all sorts of naval and military
stores, also small wooden frames of houses made in America, and
light carts, some with two, others with four wheels. These
scheming speculators have lately brought over a handsome car-
riage, hoping to barter it to advantage, but in this they have been
disappointed, although the Regent and some of the queens were
treated to a ride in it soon after it was landed. The natives still
prefer the carts where they can lie down with more ease when
they go to bathe. These carts are used but rarely on any other oc-

[19]a. In the afternoon of May 9, 1825, a party of officers from the
Blonde came ashore and marked out the first cricket ground that was
probably ever used in the isles of the Pacific. In later years the Fiji-
ans, Tongans and Samoans became very fond of cricket, playing up
to say 50 to 100 men on each side! In Hawaii cricket never caught on.
It was too slow a game and baseball is preferred.

[20]Sandalwood.

[21]This Brown was not the Captain Brown who discovered Honolulu harbor and gave it the name of Fairhaven. The latter Brown was
massacred by the natives in 1795.

[22]e.g., Cleopatra's Barge, sold to Liholiho for $90,000, payable in
sandalwood, and renamed "Haaheo o Hawaii"—"The Pride of Hawaii."
Two paintings of this vessel are exhibited in the Marine Room of the
Peabody Museum of Salem, Mass.

casion, and are drawn by natives in preference to horses or mules of which they have several on which they often ride without saddles.

BATHING THE CHIEF AMUSEMENT

Bathing is their chief amusement and alone induces many of the higher ranks of them to leave their homes, where they spend most of their time sitting or lying down asleep on mats. But the whole tribe is so fond of bathing that the sea shore is seldom seen without numbers of both sexes swimming with perfect ease, as if some speceis of aquatic creatures.

EARLY AMERICAN SETTLERS

Although the Americans have been on the islands for many years and enjoyed lucrative trade and made good fortunes, none of them have yet possessed lands of their own in this country, whether from the aversion of the chiefs to strangers or from the Americans caring only to trade in sanders wood and not take leases or grants of lands. Anyway they have but little improved the morals of the natives, and have neglected to teach them the arts of agriculture beyond what they already understood themselves when visited by Cook and Vancouver, viz., that of growing the taro root, their chief food. Even this was much neglected during the late king's reign, who, unlike his father (Tamahamaah) encouraged gambling and vices of all kinds. It is said of this late king that during his reign, till his departure for England, he inddulged in every kind of debauchery and intemperance.

LIHOLIHO AND HIS HAREM

The old Irishman who had charge of the guns at the forts, told me tales of him, and showed me the king's hut where he lived till he started for England. It was divided into two halves, one of these being again divided into separate apartmenes by low canvas screens for his six wives, who lived separately and never associated together or with the king, except one at a time. The said king had similar accommodations fitted up on a brig (the Albatross), where he sometimes went with his wives for a cruise to sea for two months together, taking the Irishman as his captain. During such a cruise he had hardly ever been free from intoxication.

The royal coffins were being cleared from the hold and were to be brought on deck the next day.

May 10. The coffins brought on deck, and those who wished, could look at the king and queen, for the outer case lids were removed. Arranged with Lord Byron and Mr. Charlton to have a hut ashore, as I could do nothing with my plants on board for want of room. Learned that the funeral would take place early the following day.

FUNERAL OF LIHOLIHO AND KAMAMALU

May 11. The coffins were lowered over the ship's side into the launch. Those going on shore to the ceremony got into boats at 1 p.m., the boats forming a line ahead of the launch to tow her ashore. Lord Byron went in his gig on the right, the first lieutenant in the whale boat on the left, with colors in all the boats hoisted half mast. On leaving the ship 26 minute guns were fired, which was continued by the same number of guns from the forts on shore and a few from an American ship in harbour. The procession of boats towing the bodies had a grand and solemn appearance. On landing, the coffins were placed on two light four-wheeled carts, covered with native black tapa cloth, the head ends of the coffin in view, and drawn side by side by their late majesties' favorite domestics, preceded by our marines and the band playing slow marches. Next after the wagons came his present majesty, supported on the right by Lord Byron and on the left by Mr. Charlton, the British consul, all in full uniform.

After these came the lieutenant and gunroom messmates and the queens in black, but many of the latter without shoes and stockings. I followed with some passengers, and then the lower rank natives and at the end about 100 sailors, four deep, with a midshipman right and left. Thus we advanced between a line of native soldiers with rusty arms reversed, naked except for the maro, save a few that had on Russian military jackets and six on each side wore handsome coloured feather tippets. These twelve we concluded must be of higher rank. The five large feather plumes, used on the day of introduction, were carried before the band in a leaning posture, as they do when going into battle.

The procession halted at the missionaries' chapel, where our chaplain read a prayer in English, and then one of the missionaries did the same in the native language. Resuming our way, the procession reached Mr. Pitt's hut, between two and three o'clock. The marines formed a line in front outside the hut. The weighty coffins were taken from the wagons by the sailors and deposited on a platform inside the hut. Here the queens of the deceased king, joined by three of his father's still alive, and who are of higher rank, stood at the head of the coffins, and were joined by the wives and daughters of the chiefs forming a line on one side of the hut. Pitt, Boki[23] and other chiefs of conse-

Boke

quence were admitted, together with the principal officers of the Blonde and a few Americans. No inferior class of natives were admitted nor had been allowed to join in the procession.

Then the chaplain gave out an anthem. It was accompanied by the band. A prayer followed, then the same performance by a missionary in the native tongue. Pitt, who had never joined the procession, remained at home in his arm chair, as usual dressed in black.

The whole ceremony was conducted with solemnity from the time of leaving the Blonde to the finish. One mistake, however, had been made. No invitation had been given to the few respectable Americans resident in the place; why is best known to those who had the conducting of the funeral, for they were left to form a small body by themselves on one side, away from the procession. It could not have been the wish of the chiefs, for they were seen often on their way to leave their places and join the Americans, especially Boki.

On the conclusion of the ceremony, all belonging to the ship were ordered back to their boats in marching order, with the band

[23]Boki, Boke or rather Poki, younger brother of Kalanimoku. He and his wife Liliha accompanied Liholiho to England. In "A Visit to the South Seas," the Rev. C. S. Stewart mentions that when he revisited Honolulu in 1829, he found "the neat wooden building erected near the fort by the regent Kaahumanu, and occupied by Lord Byron during his visit, had been removed into the town, on the level ground, some distance from the water, near Mr. Jones; and, fitted with green blinds, a flagstaff and lookout, stands a conspicuous object, both from the water and on shore, as the Blonde Hotel, owned by Governor Boki."

KALANIMOKU

(Billy Pitt)

Drawn from life by L. Choris

in front playing lively tunes. The natives broke through their soldiers' guard and clustered around us, evincing great astonishment at the great drum, and accompanying us to the harbour, where the ship's company were served with grog, and the officers had similar refreshment at Lord Byron's house. By five p.m. all were safely back on board. Mr. Dampier, the draftsman, had been stationed at an early hour where he could best make a drawing of the funeral procession,[24] and is said to have already begun taking portraits of some of the queens with whom he has taken up his residence among them at their homes.

BOTANIZES IN NUUANU VALLEY

May 12. Had permission from Lord Byron to go on shore to collect; also the favour of a lad from the ship to assist. Took some salt provisions, biscuits and my bedding on shore at 3 p.m. Stored these at first in one of the rooms of a wooden house apportioned to Lord Byron during his stay, but afterwards I went to the hut of one of the natives (Mamaware[25]), brought out with us from England, who had begged me that when he got home I would consider his house my home. On my applying for the fulfilment of his promise, he coolly forgot all about his obligations to me, and told me he knew of no hut for me, but that perhaps Pitt might find me one.

I then went on board Mr. Charlton's vessel[26] where he resided in preference to living on shore, but was again deeply disappointed, as he had Lord Byron and others at the time on board to dinner. When I met Mr. A. Bloxam,[27] who wanted to accompany me to the woods, and he proposed that we should both lodge in Lord Byron's house for the night.

May 13. Got up at 4 a.m., called the lad (Mantle) and by 5 we were ready for our journey, taking salt beef and biscuits

[24]Some of the drawings by Robert Dampier, artist on board the Blonde, appeared in the volume called An Account of the Voyage of the Blonde, which was compiled by a Mrs. Maria Graham. The same views and portraits of Hawaiian chiefs were also published in portfolio form.

[25]Manuia.

[26]The schooner Active, belonging to Capt. Richard Charlton, on board which he traded throughout the Pacific. It was this vessel that brought the Rev. Wm. Ellis to Honolulu, February 4th, 1823, on his second visit from Tahiti.

[27]Andrew Bloxom acted as a sort of amateur naturalist on the Blonde, while his brother Rowland Bloxom was the ship's chaplain.

with us and one of Mr. Charlton's asses to carry our packs. Mantle had charge of the ass. He could neither ride, drive nor lead the ass fast enough to keep up with us. It was therefore agreed to cast the ass adrift, leaving the pack saddle in one of the native huts. In crossing over the taro ponds to get to the woods, except being surrounded by low stone walls for several miles, I did not notice any difference in their cultivation from those I had seen at the island of Mowee. Here perhaps the ponds were rather better weeded. After having travelled for three miles we came to a fine, clear stream, where we halted to breakfast. We were surrounded by crowds of natives from the neighboring huts, who sat down on their hams, with us in the middle. They looked like so many starved dogs, staring at each mouthful of beef or biscuit that we took. Hoping to shame them away, we gave several of them food, but it only caused crowds to come till at last we had to tie up our provisions and move on.

During the time we stopped at the rvier, I gathered two specimens of polypodiums and three of convolvulus, besides a hibiscus with flowers, white inside and light purple out. We had not gone far, still followed by a number of natives, when we came on a chief digging up sweet potatoes. He addressed us in English and was very friendly, and on hearing of the object of our journey he gave Mr. Bloxom a young active boy to carry his traps till our return to town.

By 10 we began to enter the woods, having travelled about five miles most of the way through taro ponds and cultivated patches of sweet potatoes, bananas, water melons, etc., and in places near the river, a few low, unhealthy bread fruit trees, not in bearing.

OKOLEHAO IN 1825.

The tea tree (*dracaena*) of the country grew in all places, uncultivated in abundance. It was 2 to 4 feet high and about 1½ inches in diameter. Beyond the provision grounds, where it grew in great abundance, were sheds where the chiefs, during the last king's reign, had been in the habit of distilling great quantities of spirits from the fermented liquor made from the roots, by means of large iron try-pots obtained from whale ships in exchange for provisions.[28]

[28]The art of distilling spirituous liquors from ti (dracaena) root is said to have been introduced into Hawaii before 1800. Under the

BIRDS AND BLOSSOMS IN NUUANU VALLEY

On entering the woods we met with two trees of the *Eugenia malaccensis,* on which were a number of birds sucking its red blossoms.   Mr. B. had the luck to shoot one of them, which he said was a species of humming bird.[29]   My meeting with this kind of rose-apple, apparently growing here indigenous, so far from habitations, rather surprised me in the Sandwich Islands.   The other trees seen were common,—aleurites, and a species of acacia, used by the natives for making their canoes and paddles.   On the ground below were mixed a variety of handsome ferns in all kind of places, moist and dry.   Further towards the centre of the island, the trees became more lofty and the ground below them more shady and damp, where there appeared several species of *Psychotrias* and *Beselerias* with two or three tall-growing *Lobelias* with splendid clusters of flowers.   There were also three kinds of *Metrosideros* with rich bunches of scarlet flowers.   These were covered with birds, sucking honey from the blossoms, which we shot, but could not afterwards find, owing to the thick growth of ferns, plants, etc.

NUUANU PALI

We gained the head of the valley at 5 p.m., having travelled about ten miles, when we had a splendid view of the Pacific Ocean on both sides of the island. Here we had a cool breeze, occasioned by the valley terminating in a narrow gap, overhung on each side by high abrupt cliffs covered with tufts of *lycopodium cernum,* so common within the tropics, and two or three kinds of *vaccini-ums,* besides other low shrubby plants which clothe this mountain, at least 3000 feet to its summit, with pleasant verdure. At this point there is a path which leads down to the valley on the other side of the island.

18th amendment to the U. S. Constitution, the manufacture of all kinds of spirituous or malt liquors is made illegal in the United States, of which Hawaii now forms a part. Notwithstanding this, the illicit distillation of spirits made from rice, pineapples, maize, etc., is carried on to a much greater extent than in former years, and during the year 1921 over $60,000 in fines were collected in Hawaii from transgressors of the prohibition law. The distillation of spirits from ti root was introduced into Tahiti in 1798 by two Sandwich Islanders who had deserted from the British N.W. Coast fur trader Nautilus.

[29]There are no humming birds in the Hawaiian Islands.

While we were at this place, which is a thoroughfare for the natives crossing the island, we were surprised to be overtaken by a man, better dressed than the rest of the natives, who accosted us in English and very familiarly entered into conversation. He told us he was a native of Otahiti, which he had left when a boy to serve on a whale ship. Afterwards he was in the British navy, till he was wounded at the battle of Algiers, when he was discharged as unfit for service with a pension of twenty-five pounds a year. Having learned from this man that we could travel by the sea coast round the east side of the island to the town next day, we decided to remain in some hut for the night. But in order to advance farther, we had to make the most difficult descent to the bottom of the precipice by a winding rocky path, in places for several yards together quite perpendicular. We had to take off our shoes and to scramble as best we could, at times backwards on our hands and knees. The natives in our company carried their loads seemingly with perfect ease, and enjoyed heartily seeing us in the least terror to go on, coming to our assistance to prevent our falling. Fortunately we got to the bottom without any accident, and soon came to two or three small huts where we obtained lodgings for the night in the hut of a Bengal black, who had been wrecked in an Indiaman on the coast some years ago, and had since then lived on the island with a native woman, by whom he had several children. He spoke good English, and told us he was a tailor, and sometimes acted as cook for the king before he went to England.

VISITS KANEOHE

As it was not yet dark, we proposed a walk to the sea side, about 1½ miles distant, while our host cooked us supper. On our way we passed several native huts with little patches of cultivated ground, chiefly planted with Brousonettia, from the bark of which they make the tapa cloths. They also cultivate a plant which they name None,[30] for the sake of its fruit, which yields their favorite yellow dye for the tapa cloths. In the hollows were some taro ponds and several groves of healthy trees of the rose apple, growing apparently without any cultivation and coming into fruit. The bay is open and exposed and full of rocks in many places above water, which renders it unsafe for vessels to anchor. It is full of fish.

[30]Noni (Morinda citrifolia), a plant found throughout Polynesia, Malaysia, etc.

The high ridge of mountains which runs nearly in the centre of the island, terminates on this side in high abrupt cliffs. Along the coast for four or five miles back into the interior, the country is, as in the neighborhood of Hanarura, left everywhere uncultivated as nature had formed it, excepting the small patches round the native huts. Although there is good pasture, none of the government cattle have yet been sent to this side from Hanarura to feed.

On our return we found some taro root ready baked under ground with hot stones, and a small fresh water fish of the mullet kind cooked in the same way, enclosed in the leaf of a tea tree. We slept on mats by the side of the Bengal black and his wife, with her father and mother and the rest of the family, in all, upwards of a dozen men, women and children, besides several dogs, thickly stowed together at one end of the hut without distinction.

May 14. ¦Got up at 4 a.m., after a restless night from fleas and cold, the hut being so open that light could be seen through it. Informed by our landlord that going round the island, as we intended and were told by the Otahitian, would take but one day, would, in reality, take two days. For want of provisions, we were reluctantly obliged to return by the road we had come. We left our host at 5 a.m., the dew still on the grass, after giving him a trifle for his last night's trouble.

CLIMBS THE NUUANU PALI

We overtook a number of natives at the precipice, which we had found so difficult to descend. Most of the natives were loaded with provisions for the chiefs, such as large hogs, tied together by the four feet and carried on the back, at other times led or driven. Others with bundles of taro or large calabashes of poi, secured to each end of a staff thrown across the shoulder, and travelling thus with a short shuffling step, stopping to rest themselves every now and then, and to have a draw in turn from a wooden tobacco pipe, and then resume their journey as before.

TATOOING AND HAIR DRESSING

They have no calculation of time, beyond the rising and setting of the sun, and only care to gain some hut for the night, being too superstitious to travel after dark. Both sexes are generally tatooed irregularly, with figures of goats, muskets and even letters of the alphabet. Name and birthplace with date of the year are often seen tatooed along the arm. Many of the men shave their heads, and cut their hair in the form of a helmet, the crest of which is often stained with lime, so as to be of a light whitish colour. The women esteem it cut short, with a rim over the forehead bleached white and standing up in front like bristles. Sometimes a long curl is preserved in the middle of the forehead, which is combed backwards. Some suffer their hair to grow and tie it up behind in a bunch. Many of the females, different from any of the other sex, have a tatooed line about two inches broad inside the thigh down as low as the ankle, where it terminates in the form of a ring generally on the right foot. Most of them had a looking glass and a wooden tobacco pipe tied round the neck in a handkerchief or piece of tapa cloth. They are very fond of smoking, and are seldom seen without a pipe, and curiously enough the habit among them is, though most of both sexes have and carry a pipe, for one of them to light his or her pipe, and after a few draws by the person who filled it, to pass it along without distinction of persons, until all have had a draw at it.

By ten o'clock we were nearly through the wood, when Mr. B., impatient of waiting for us, parted from us, he to return home before the sun's heat increased, while I remained behind in order to collect more plants not met with yesterday. When I arrived in Hanarura, I found that no place had been arranged for me, while I am out in the woods. Got all my traps moved on board and lay out my plant specimens on paper.

May 15. Sunday. Church service on board at 10. Spent most of the day laying out specimens, sorting seed, etc. The surveyor, purser and midshipman, in the whale boat, were upset in the surf going on shore, and had a twenty minutes ducking, till another boat went to their assistance.

May 16. Went on shore with Mr. Forder, who intends to remain ashore and draw plants, and take care of the hut provided for me, while I am out in the woods. Got all my traps moved into my hut, which is about half a mile east of the town, and has never been tenanted before. Shifted my specimens, while Mantle slung our hammocks across the corners of the hut. Before dusk, Lord Byron and the surgeon rode out to ask if I would care to go with them and a party to Pearl River by water, and if so, had better breakfast with them at 8 a.m.

TRIP TO PEARL RIVER OR HARBOUR

May 17. Joined Lord Byron's party, with Mantle carrying my traps. We did not embark until noon. After two hours

TATOOED HAWAIIAN CHIEF

Playing the game of balancing on stone ball

sailing along the coast, we entered the mouth of the Pearl River, which divides itself into several branches, forming two islands. One which is smaller than the other is called Rabbit island, from a person, the name of Marine, a Spaniard, residing at Hanarura, having put rabbits on it some years ago. The rabbits have since increased in numbers.

It became so calm, that his Lordship, Mr. C., and the Bloxoms left us in the launch, and rowed in the small boat in tow, and soon disappeared from sight. We waited in suspense, hour after hour, not knowing the several branches of the river, nor where we were to spend the night. The boat party pulling into one branch of the river, the other in which I was tacking about from bank to bank till the boaters hauled their boat ashore and we cast anchor. Both parties were opposite each other on Rabbit Island, but ignorant of the fact, till on walking about the island, the parties met. One hut was noticed, and those on the island made for it, but the launch having the ladies and some others on board, got up anchor and sailed round to the hut, where with the help of canoes, they all landed. The ladies were somewhat discontented, but after a good dinner partaken sitting on mats spread on the grass, harmony was restored.

At dusk we embarked to cross to a larger hut. Landed at 8 p.m. At ten o'clock two old men entered our hut to play the hura dance on a couple of bottle shaped gourds. They took a sitting posture, beating time on the gourds with the palms of their hands, accompanied by a song made up about the late king.

About 11, we all retired to rest, lying down beside each other on mats, some with pumpkins or what else they could get for a pillow. The ladies got themselves screened off in a corner with a flag without any other accommodation.

Pearl River is about seven miles west of Hanarura, and is improperly called a river, being rather inlets from the sea, branching off in different directions. There are three chief branches, named by the surveyors, the East, Middle and West Lochs. The entrance to Pearl River is very narrow and shallow, and in its present state it is fit for very small vessels to enter, but over the bar there is deep water, and in the channel leading to the lochs there are from 7 to 20 fathoms. The lochs themselves are rather shallow.

The coast from Hanarura to the west of Pearl River possesses no variety of plants beyond two or three species, such as

Argemones, Portulacas, and a few other little annuals, intermixed with the common long grass so plentiful everywhere on the coast round the island.

OYSTERS

The oysters that are found in Pearl River are small and insipid and of no value or consequence.

RETURNS BY LAND

May 18. Got up at 4 a.m., after a restless night, having been tormented with fleas. Departed with my man Mantle, leaving the rest yet asleep. But after travelling about three miles, the path which we had first struck terminated, and the grass became longer and more difficult to travel over. At last, after another three miles, we got so entangled with creeping plants running a little above the ground beneath the grass, that Mantle, who was stockingless, shed tears, complaining of his ankles, and refused to go on. Being yet five miles from the woods, and not having sufficient provisions for two days, we were forced to return to the town by a path leading through taro ponds, some distance inland from the coast.

On the path we had left near the Pearl River, we saw several thickly inhabited huts, situated on the side of a ravine stocked with bananas, taro and healthy breadfruit trees just forming their fruit. Here we met with an old Englishman, who told us there was on the opposite side of the ravine a large river coming out under the ground. We went to the place and found that what he had told us was correct, and stood admiring the subterranean stream of fine, cool water. Its source was rapid, forming a cascade nearly 20 feet in height, having ferns and mosses on its sides. In the grounds of the natives, I saw plenty of the awa plant (*piper*) mentioned in the history of these islands, as being destructive to the health of the natives when used to excess, owing to its intoxicating qualities. I obtained several specimens of it in flower.

The old man informed me that he had been on the island over sixteen years, and that the grounds we were then upon, belonged to Boki, and had been in his charge for ten years. Upon Boki going to England with the king, another chief had turned him away, and taken all his little ground from him, so that he had been forced to live on the charity of the natives.

EWA DISTRICT

The neighbourhood of the Pearl River is very extensive, rising backwards with a gentle slope towards the woods, but is without cultivation, except round the outskirts to about half a mile from the water. The country is divided into separate farms or allotments belonging to the chiefs, and enclosed with walls from four to six feet high, made of a mixture of mud and stone. The poorer natives live on these farms, also a few ragged foreigners who have a hut with a small spot of ground given them, for which they must work for the chiefs a certain number of days besides paying an annual rent in dogs, hogs, goats, poultry and tapa cloths, which they have to carry to whatever spot their master is then living on the island. On the least neglect to perform these demands, they are turned away and deprived of whatever stock, etc., they may possess. Such is the present despotic or absolute law in the Sandwich Islands. This is corroborated by all foreigners met with at different times, who, on our arrival, hoped that Lord Byron would render them their little property more secure in future. Unfortunately they must wait till the British Consul helps them, as we have no authority to interfere with the laws of the country.

On our way home we noticed that the country on the side towards the woods still remained uncultivated, also towards the sea coast, except the lower ends of the small valleys which are cultivated with the taro in ponds, which much resemble peat mosses that had been worked and afterwards allowed to get full of stagnant water. There is no convenient road to travel anywhere on the island. We met with another subterranean river at the side of one of the hollows, larger than the other, but of no great fall after its appearance from underground.

MOANALUA HILL

By 4 p.m. we gained the summit of a high hill, thickly covered with tufts of long grass. It lies within three miles of Hanarura. There is a burying ground of the natives at the top, which was formerly where the chiefs of high rank had a morai.[31] At the bottom towards the sea, there is a circular salt pond,[32] nearly two miles in circumference, surrounded by low conical hills. In

[31] In Hawaiian "heiau."

[32] Known as Aliapaakai.

places on the sides of a valley leading to the pond from the interior, are several huts of the natives with taro ponds and a large grove of coco-nut trees, apparently very old from their great height and mossy appearance. We reached town about six o'clock having travelled twenty miles since morning without much success, being too near the coast to meet with a variety of plants. We learnt, however, a good deal about the present mode of life of the natives, and the manner in which they continue to cultivate their grounds, differing but little, if any, from the descriptions given by Capt. Cook and others.

May 19. Fine. Saw to my specimens. Lord Byron and the surgeon called to hear particulars of my journey home from Pearl River. American missionaries called and invited me to return the visit. Mantle still complained of his feet, but will go in the morning to the woods with me. Mr. Bloxam accompanied me to the woods, but by 8 a.m. he said he had shot enough birds to skin and would go home. I asked him to shoot a few for me, as he had enough for himself, but he refused, saying all his duplicates were for Lord Byron.

CLIMBS "TANTALUS" MOUNTAIN

As we advanced to the wood, we met with a multiplicity of ferns, many of them different from those I had seen on the 13th and 14th in Hanarura valley. By 12 o'clock we had gained the summit of the highest hill fronting the bay, and it rained in torrents. Here I took the temperature of the air, which stood at 69. This hill is over 2000 feet above sea level, but there are others byond it in the centre of the island of much greater height. Two miles beyond this high hill, the wood became difficult to penetrate, and being so wet, we set out homewards. The ferns of different kinds met with during the day exceed twelve. We met also with a considerable variety of plants, among which were a parasitical species of metrosideros with large scarlet flowers and two or three lobelias with handsome flowers.

LAND SHELLS

I met also for the first time with small land shells, having a variety of rich striped colours. These shells were found chiefly on the leaves of the wild tapa (*Brousonettia*) of which there are several species with different coloured flowers. At the huts near the wood, we saw some natives eating raw sweet potatoes, just taken up from the ground and not even washed.

Got home at six o'clock. Lord Byron called to say he was riding farther on towards Diamond Hill, and would I meet him the next day at Pitt's to see the plants, which had been brought out from England, properly transplanted.

EXPLORES DIAMOND HEAD OR HILL

May 21. Met Lord Byron, according to promise, at Mr. Pitt's to transplant the fruit trees brought from England, but when I got there found he had not come. After waiting some time I went to his house, and saw Mr. Charlton, who doubted if anything could be done then, as Mr. Pitt and the other chiefs were then asleep, and would not get up on any account whatever. I was advised not to wait on the chance of finishing the planting, but to go, as I had intended, to Diamond Hill. So Mantle and I set off and were joined by a native who offered himself as a guide. By 6.30 we had gained the summit, which is high and steep, without anything growing on it but tufts of dry grass in loose sand, which came up very easily and rendered the ascent more difficult. Diamond Hill forms a headland near the sea, about three miles from Hanarura, and has at some former period been an old volcanic crater, now extinct. In the centre is a level flat, two acres in size, covered with longer grass than the external declivity. On the inside part next to the sea, the depth is upwards of 500 feet, counting from the narrow ridge round the top, which is almost circular. Some parts of the rocks had the appearance of common quartz; others resembled burnt limestone, turned soft and white.

There are many natives' huts along the coast on both sides of the hill, surrounded by banana and coco-nut trees. Coco-nut trees seldom grow far from the coast. Near Hanarura is a similar crater, now a fort, with several guns placed along the ridge. A salute was fired from this fort when we entered the harbour.

On our way home, in a high wind, my hat was blown off, and Mantle went down the cliff to retrieve it. It was nearly dark and he called out to myself and the native guide not to leave him behind. Afterwards he told me that in picking up the hat, he had picked up a large human skull. At first he had not noticed what he had picked up till he saw the hollow part of the eyes, and had called out in fright and thrown the skull away. On my expostulating he said he could get plenty more, as there were

a lot there. This was explained to me by the American I had
hired as cook and who had been on the island for six years, by
his telling me that in former times, the chiefs used to take their
criminals upon the top of Diamond Hill to put them to death by
throwing them over the precipice, where they were left unburied
in the hollow, and thus Mantle had met with many skulls.

TAMAAHAMAHAA ALIAS "THE DUKE OF WELLINGTON"

May 23.   At 4 p.m., the Governor of Attooi called on me.
He was busy quelling the insurrection on that island about two
months before our arrival. He is also styled the Duke of Welling-
ton, the conqueror of Attooi.   He is a young man of about 25,
stout and good looking, in comparison to the rest of his countrymen.   He was brought up by Boki, who was in England, and formerly, until made a governor and general, went under the name
of Tamaahamahaa.   I placed before him a nearly full gin case
bottle of rum and a tumbler, which he finished by himself in less
than two hours time, and went home but very little intoxicated. I
took care, however, never to make him quite as free with my
bottle again.

VISITS MANOA VALLEY

May 24.   Went to the woods through a valley near Diamond
Hill, named by me Wilkinson's,[33] from its being the place where
the unfortunate man lived that we had brought out from England
with us in the suite of the Sandwich Islanders in the prospect of
improving the state of agriculture here.   But he found that he
had to do with ignorant, unfeeling masters, who instead of employ-
ing him to improve their farms, with a liberal salary, had only
given him some waste land in the valley to cultivate for his own,
during their own pleasure.   On passing through his land I found
he was ill in a tent, having no hut built yet.   He lay on a mat-
tress on the ground, suffering from diarrhoea, and reduced to a
skeleton, and looking the picture of death.   I suggested that he
should apply to Lord Byron for a passage home with us, but he

[33]Wilkinson is credited with having been the first person to cultivate coffee in the Hawaiian group. The first plantation was started
at the head of Manoa valley, Oahu, with seed or young plants obtained
at St. Catherines, Brazil, where H.M.S. Blonde touched on the way
out from England. Died March, 1827, before reaping the reward for
his labor.

said he would rather die where he was than return to England. His land was near the head of the valley in a kind of amphitheatre overhung by volcanic ridges, thickly covered with candle nut (*aleurites*) and other trees, that occasion much rain at night.

In several parts of this valley, I met with great quantities of turmeric, ginger, awa, and one specimen of canna, growing wild among the grass. The ginger is met with in abundance everywhere on coming to within half a mile of the woods, but afterwards it disappears on getting some miles further on. The roots are generally bitter, and have not much of the taste of cultivated ginger. When in the wood, I met with four more different species of metrosideros, and several other plants which I had not seen before. At the head of the valley at the side of a small river which descends from the mountains, are trees of the *Eugenia malaccensis*, forming a wood by themselves. On my return home I saw hundreds of the natives preparing the ground near where I lived, for Mr. Pitt, in order to be planted with sweet potatoes. They did this by pulling up the grass with their hands, and others using a short stick to loosen the ground. They have as yet no other description of tools.

TWO OF KAMEHAMEHA'S WIDOWS CALL ON MACRAE

May 25. Two of the late Tamahamaah's queens called on their way to bathe. Both of their majesties on coming to the door in a cart drawn by several natives, were tilted out without ceremony, like so much rubbish, being unable to get out in any other way, owing to their enormous size. They were dressed in Canton crapes, made in European fashion, with coarse straw bonnets and old slippers, but no stockings.

Mr. Forder to amuse them, showed the drawings of plants, etc., that he had made, and they asked to be given them all, and when refused, they asked for something else. They are very covetous. When they went, they got into the cart, laid hold of the front part standing up together behind, and in this manner the box (cart) was raised up with them face downwards, and their legs, nearly the size of a man's body, hanging over the hind part of the cart, which was too short for their length.

LOOKS FOR SANDAL WOOD

May 26. Showers of rain. Went to the valley above Diamond Hill looking for sanders wood. It is this kind of wood which has bestowed so much wealth on its owner, and caused the neglect of cultivation in the islands since its discovery, owing to the natives being taken away from their homes for weeks together to procure it.

In the wood at the head of this valley, I met with many plants not seen before, particularly ferns and metrosideros. The latter formed the greatest number of the largest trees I had seen, except the acacia from which the native canoes are made. The sanders wood I met with grew only to a middling sized tree, and was too early in the season for flowering. In the forest, bananas grow wild to a great size, with many large bunches of fruit on them, which the natives with me cut and roasted. One which I tasted was bitter, but by no means unpalatable. The fruit of the wild banana is the chief food of the natives when they are in the woods collecting sanders wood or for the purpose of rough-hewing their canoes light enough to enable them to drag them to the sea shore. This latter operation often takes several days.

NATIVE METHOD OF OBTAINING FIRE

Today for the first time I saw the natives light a fire to roast their bananas, by rubbing two dried sticks upon each other, that catch fire by friction, after rubbing them for about a minute.

May 27. Fine, but showery. Hearing that the ship would sail in a few days for Owyhee, I went to Lord Byron to ascertain if he would return to this island again before he left the islands for Otahite, for if so, I must have all my plant boxes on board. He said he could only tell he was leaving in a few days.

JOHN YOUNG AND ISAAC DAVIS

He introduced me to Mr. Young. His name along with that of his companion, Mr. Davis, have long been distinguished in the history of these islands. Mr. Young had just come from Owyhee. He is now fast sinking under the infirmities of age. Mr. Davis is dead and buried in the Europeans' burying place under a grove of coco-nut trees near where I live, and on his simple monument is engraved

"The remains of Mr. Isaac Davis,
who died at this island
April 1810, aged 52 years."

On his decease, he had possessed many lands or farms in the different islands, given him by Tamahamaah for his faithful services, which afterwards became the property of his wife and

JOHN YOUNG

("Olohana"—"All hands.")

The friend and Companion-in-Arms of Kamehameha.
Born Lancashire, England, 1742; died Honolulu, December 17, 1835.
Aged 93 years.

daughters, but some have lately been taken from them by some of the covetous chiefs now in power.

MAGIC LANTERN SHOW BANNED BY MISSIONARIES

Lord Byron had a magic lantern show at the king's hut, but owing to the religious fanaticism of the American Methodists, the king was prevented from being present.[34] These missionaries, many of them being but illiterate mechanics, possess what power they please over the credulity of the natives, and have already carried their system of religion too far to be upheld.

PLANTS BROUGHT FROM ENGLAND

May 28. Met Mr. Charlton at 6 a.m. at Mr. Pitt's hut to see, transplanted, the plants that were brought out from England. I found the natives had already finished planting out the tropical plants, among which I had several *Orchidacae* from St. Catharines, doing very well in their box. Although my *Orchidacae* intended for Mr. Lindley[35] were now partly destroyed, my feelings at the moment were nothing compared to what they were when I saw the natives tear up my other plants by the stems, as a gardener would cabbage stumps for the dung heap. Mr. Charlton was not present, so I requested Mr. Pitt to stop having anything done until I returned with the Consul, at which Mr. Pitt only laughed at my eagerness.

MARIN (MANINI) THE SPANIARD

When I returned, I found that self-conceited Spaniard, Marin, helping to pull the plants by the stems, and continued doing so in my presence. I remonstrated, but Mr. Charlton drew me to one side and said "I had better leave the fellow to himself to do with the plants as he thought proper," to which I agreed, on condition

[34]In regard to this magic lantern incident, the missionaries' side of the question may be learned by consulting the following works, viz., "An Examination of Charges against the American Missionaries at the Sandwich Islands as alleged in the Voyage of the Ship Blonde and in the London Quarterly Review," Cambridge, Mass., 1827; also "A Defence of the Missions in the South Sea and Sandwich Islands, etc.," by William Orme. London, 1827.

[35]John Lindley, the well known English botanist and horticulturist, who during his lifetime was the mainspring of the Horticultural Society of London. It was under the auspices of this society that Macrae had been sent out in charge of a variety of plants to be distributed at the Sandwich Islands.

that Mr. Charlton would explain to strangers touching here that I had no hand in the transplanting. I then took up my St. Catherines Orchidacae and replanted them in the box from which they had been taken, and then proceeded to make a list of what plants had been introduced alive, but found the natives had stolen all the leaden numbers attached to each plant, as well as the iron hooks that kept the lids of the boxes open when the plants required air on the passage from England.

ALEXANDER ADAMS

May 29. Sunday. Fine. Went with our purser to the house of the harbour pilot (Mr. Adams) to accompany them to the other side of the island, to see the steep cliffs where I and Mr. A.B. had difficulty in passing on the 13th. Mr. Adams amused us throughout the day relating curious anecdotes of the late Tamahamaah and his queens, particularly about Kaumanna. Adams had been on the islands since 1809,[36] sometimes conveying sanders wood to China, at other times to the North-West coasts of America with cargoes of salt. He brought home a couple of deer[37] the last time with a view of their thriving in the islands, but they

[36]It was owing to the intercession of three British seamen, viz., Alexander Adams, John Young and Isaac Davis, who had been trusted councillors of Kamehameha I, and who had been continued in the same capacity by his son Liholiho, that the first contingent of American missionaries, after being confined on board the Thaddeus at Kailua in 1820 for two weeks, were finally allowed by Liholiho and his council of chiefs to land and settle on the islands. In the Sandwich Islands Magazine for 1856, page 78, Judge Abraham Fornander, the leading Hawaiian historian, gives his opinion on this point as under, viz., "Though all these probably had an influence more or less determining the decision of the king and queen-regent, yet after all the most direct influence that decided this admission of the missionaries and their permanent residence, was the intercession of a few Englishmen, long resident on the islands, and without whose names any account of the first period of Hawaiian civilization would be imperfect and unintelligible. That their names have not yet had honorable mention in this connection by those who have assumed to write on Hawaiian history, is one of the sins of omission which we would charitably overlook if we could. Those men were Young, Davis and Adams. The two first were settled here before, and contributed in no small degree to the conquest and its results; the latter is still living to reap that tribute of respect, that tardy justice, which those who have neglected to render, whom he and the others assisted in their hour of need and cheered in their moments of doubt."

[37]Deer were not the only kind of wild animals introduced into Honolulu during the reign of Liholiho. In 1822, that monarch dispatched his American-built brig, the Sunbeam, commanded by an Eng-

CAPTAIN ALEXANDER ADAMS,
Designer of the Hawaiian Flag.

Born at Arbroath, Scotland, December 27, 1780.
Died at Honolulu, October 27, 1871.
Aged 91 years.

had not long been suffered to go at large in Hanarura valley, when Pitt happening to be unwell, fancied that the flesh of the deer would do him good, and one of them was killed for him to taste. This he found so much to his liking that he ordered the other one to be killed, thus ending the life of poor Adams' deer.

BATTLE OF NUUANU VALLEY

On our way through the valley of Hanarura or Nuanu, as it is often called, we were shown the spot where the king of Woahoo's (Tereaboo) head general was killed after the invasion of Tamahamaah from Owhyee to conquer the island. It happened as follows: When Tamahamaah with Young and Davis and the rest of his army had landed from their small fleet in the harbour, without opposition from Tereaboo, they found that the latter had collected his forces above the town in Hanarura valley. Tamahamaah could not have wished for a better situation or one more favourable to his purpose, the valley being overhung by ridges on each side, which were left unoccupied by the enemy. Tamahamaah, without any opposition from the enemy, placed a number of his men on the side ridges, and then he himself, accompanied by Young, Davis and the greater part of his army, took up their position in the center of the valley. They had with them only one small swivel and a few firearms, the rest being armed with spears and clubs. Mr. Davis, who had the swivel, somewhat singular to relate, killed Tereaboo's general on his firing the first shot, before the engagement had scarcely begun. When this happened, as is usual with these natives, they instantly got into confusion and retreated. Tamahamaah pursued them up the valley, and on coming to the precipice they threw themselves over and were found in the thousands, lifeless at the bottom of the cliff.

lishman, Captain John Bowles, and manned by Sandwich Islanders, to St. Peter and St. Pauls (Petropaulovski), Kamtschatka, with a cargo of salt as a present to his imperial brother, the Czar of Russia. In return for this gift on the part of the Sandwich Islands king, the governor of St. Peter and St. Paul's, who was then Captain Ricord, an Englishman, gave such articles as seemed most desirable, including some animals, with a view of propagating the breed. Amongst the animals were two Siberian bears, but what became of them when landed at Honolulu is now forgotten. Some details about this voyage of the Sunbeam in search of bears will be found in Captain John Dundas Cochrane, R.N.'s, "Narrative of a Pedestrian Journey," etc. 2nd ed. London 1824, pp. 425-7, and an amusing sketch called "Kamehameha II's Bears," by a Russian author, V. Poliakoff, appeared in Chambers' Journal for 1st March, 1920.

Thus did Tamahamaah, with the help of Young and Davis, and with hardly any firearms, easily conquer this important island, which may now be considered the first of the Sandwich Islands on account of its good harbour. The king of Woahoo fled to the mountains, being convinced that the custom of putting the vanquished to death would be practiced upon him. "I must die," he said to one of his friends, "for I will not let Tamahamaah enjoy this triumph. I will sacrifice myself to the gods." His corpse was afterwards found in a cave in the mountains.[38]

I managed to shoot some birds, one being particularly handsome. Its feathers were all red,[39] and it is only met with when sucking the red blossoms of the metrosideros.

May 30. Fine, with light showers of rain. Therm. 6 a.m., 76; 12 noon, 86; 7 p.m., 76.

ALEXANDER ADAMS HELPS MACRAE

May 31. Went with Mr. Charlton and Mr. Pitt to get my empty plant boxes taken to a carpenter to be repaired. Pitt promised natives to help, but none came, so in despair, I went to Mr. Charlton to go with me to procure assistance for which I was willing to pay rather than waste more time. However we met Mr. Adams, the pilot, who kindly borrowed a cart and got his own people and came with them and we soon got the whole lot of boxes removed.

The plants brought from England had remained without any shade from the sun. Through the neglect of these people, I found only one grape vine with any leaves on it. Plants which at the expense of the Horticultural Society, had been brought 15,000 miles by sea through various climates: Marin, the Spaniard, previously mentioned, has had a grape vine since 1814, which he

[38]This account of the death of King Kalanikupule differs from that given by Fornander in the Polynesian Race Vol. II, p. 348. There it is stated that the king was captured in the mountains of Waipio, Oahu, brought to Kamehameha and sacrificed to the latter's god Kukailimoku. Probably the truth is that Kalanikupule's corpse was found in a cave by those hunting for him, and brought to Honolulu, where it would be offered up as an offering to Kamehameha's god.

[39]The Iiwi (Vestiaria coccinea) or the apapane (Himatione sanguinea). Native birds are getting very scarce on Oahu and the other islands of the group. About 1910, or so, the writer noticed on two or three occasions, an iiwi in his garden situated on Prospect Street, on the south side of Punchbowl Hill. This is about one-third of a mile from the business centre of Honolulu.

brought from California, where he had been with Adams as lin-
guist, and had planted in his own ground near Hanarura,[40] and
got the king to perform the charm of taboo to prevent any being
stolen. This taboo still continues in force to the present time,
but although he has cultivated the vine with success for the last
two years, and made more than two casks of wine from the
fruit, sooner than give the slips to his neighbors, he has burnt the
prunings every year.

But Mr. Charlton has given to different individuals, several
fine grape vines which he brought with him from the port of Valparaiso, and also an assortment of vegetable seeds, the gift of the
Horticultural Society, London. Mr. Charlton intends soon to
reside with his family at Woahoo, where he intends to grow coffee
and cotton, which have so far been neglected. In such a favourable climate, they, as well as cocoa and sugar, may be brought to
perfection.

QUEEN KAAHUMANU

June 1. Returning from the town, I saw Queen Kaumana
in her four-wheeled cart being dragged to the top of a small hill
by natives. The cart was afterwards pushed off at the top and
allowed to roll down hill by itself, with her in it. This ludicrous
sort of amusement was always accompanied with much shouting
on the part of the natives.

June 2. Queen Kaumanna and Pio,[41] with several female
attendants, called in their carts. They were very inquisitive to
know if Mr. Forder and I were married men. Being told, yes,
they wanted to know the number in our families. Mr. Forder,
who kept up the conversation, said he had six and I none, on
which they said I could only have one wife. After a few more
questions, they left us to bathe, as usual, in the fish pond, near
here.

A little before dusk, the king called on horseback, accompanied by a little boy brought out from England by Boki. His
majesty was dressed in a short blue jacket and pantaloons to
match, but without hat, waistcoat, shoes or stockings. Afterwards
we saw his sister, the young princess, carried home from bathing

[40]At Pauoa Valley.
[41]Piia, alias Lydia Namahana, sister of Kaahumanu.

on a native boy's back, some distance in front of the old queens, who were dragged in the carts.

June 3. The ship sails for Owhyee on the 7th, so I am instructed to have my traps on board again this evening. Packed up my specimens and got everything on board by dusk.

June 4. Got my things stowed away amidst the usual noise of a man-o'-war. At 5 p.m., one of the gentlemen hooked a shark alongside which measured 11 feet in length and five in circumference, and when cut open, in its stomach were found a large hook and chain carried away the day before, a bullock's foot, part of a pig's head, and many bones which had been thrown over the ship's side, where he had been noticed for several days past. The Sandwich people who were going with us to Owhyee sent on board a quantity of luggage and provisions for their passage.

June 5. Sunday. Fine. Church service on board as usual at 10 a.m.

June 6. Went on shore. In the town saw a large pig roasted with hot stones in the way customary with the South Sea Islanders, and as mentioned by Capt. Cook and others.

WOMEN SUCKLE PIGS AND DOGS

Shortly afterwards, I noticed a young woman walking along the street, and at the same time suckling several puppies that were wrapped up in a piece of tapa cloth hanging round her shoulders and breasts. The custom of suckling dogs and pigs is common to the natives of the Sandwich Islands. These animals are held by them in great estimation, little inferior to their own offspring, and my journeys to the woods in search of plants often afforded me an opportunity of being an eye witness to this habit. I often saw them feeding the young pigs and dogs with the poi made from the taro root, in the same way as a mother would her child.

The dogs are in general useless for anything but being eaten, and are seldom ever heard to bark. In size they are small, with long bodies and ears, sharp pricked noses and short feet. They are mostly black in colour, but very often hairless from mange. In this state the natives feed them and preserve their offspring, which they carry in their arms oftener than they do their own young. In passing their huts, should a stranger hurt one of their dogs, they are more offended than if one of their own children had been attacked.

BOKI and LILIHA

From drawing by
Sir George Hayter, P.R.A.

MEETING TO CONSIDER NEW LAWS

At 2 p.m., a meeting was held at Pitt's house, of Lord Byron and all the chiefs, to consider fit laws to be established throughout the islands. Boki stood up for half an hour and made a surprising speech. His own countrymen were so astonished, they said it must be someone else in Boki's skin. He compared what he had seen in England with his own country, and strongly recommended them to establish laws and religion on the English principles. He wished fires to be allowed in their houses to cook on Sunday, and also to be allowed to bathe on Sundays as in England. After discussion, however, it was resolved that the former laws of Tamahamaah should be again put in force.

MARINES TOO DRUNK TO DRILL

At 3 p.m., the marines came on shore to go through movements for Pitt's gratification, but unfortunately several got intoxicated on their way through town and could not go through the affair to Lord Byron's disappointment, for most of the royal family and the chiefs and European residents were present.[42]

WILKINSON. NOVARA'S INN

Wilkinson, now much better, was there, and was anxious to get Lord Byron to obtain a promise from Pitt that the land given him should not be taken from him, but this Pitt and the chiefs will not promise, only saying "He could have it until the ground may be wanted by themselves."

I stayed the night in the inn of Novara,[43] in company with the assistant surgeon.

[42]History repeats itself. In 1825, the British marines apparently got pretty well loaded up with okolehao (native gin). Nearly a century afterwards, the same scene was being enacted in Honolulu. According to a Honolulu newspaper of April 4, 1921, "Fifty-two (U.S.) soldiers were brought to the police station, Honolulu, Saturday night and early Sunday morning. This establishes a record for a single night's arrest of soldiers. They were brought in individually and in groups, practically all being under the influence of liquor, according to the police." This happened in "dry" America.

[43]Novara's inn was situated on the "mauka" side of what is now called Merchant Street, nearly opposite the present police station. Joseph Novara died at Honolulu, 14th February, 1839, aged 72. Was a sailor by profession ,and had lived in Honolulu for over 30 years.

QUEEN KAAHUMANU, JOHN YOUNG AND CHIEFS
SAIL ON THE BLONDE

June 7. Lord Byron informed me I need not send my empty plant boxes on board, as he intended to touch here again. Queen Kaumanna and Pio, with Mr. Young and several chiefs and other natives came on board to go with us to Heddo Bay, situate on the east side of Owhyee.

Took leave of Mr. Charlton, with hopes of seeing him again at Otahite on our way home. Got under weigh at 3 p.m. Fresh breeze from E.N.E. Among the queen's attendants was an old cunning fellow, "Jack Bligh," native of Otahite, who spoke a little English, and had, he said, been with Captain Bligh in the Bounty at the time of the mutiny. We had on board also two missionaries and "Sir Joseph Banks," interpreter to Lord Byron.

June 8. Fine. Fresh breezes from the N.E. At noon the island of Mowee in sight. Therm. 6 a.m. 76; 12 noon 75; 7 p.m. 76.

June 9. Being near the island of Mowee, a boat was sent on shore with Joe Banks, to procure fish. He returned with a quantity, fresh and salted, which the natives immediately began to devour raw, with some poi and taro, not even wasting their gills or entrails. These parts are considered by them to be the most delicate parts of the fish, and were what was generally eaten by the queens and chiefs. Among others doing this was Manaware,[44] whom we had brought out from England. When I, disgusted, expostulated and told him he ought to have shown his countrymen how he had seen us eat our meals, he replied, somewhat offended, that he and his countrymen liked fish in that way best, adding that "He saw plenty of poor people in England, but we see none here; that they got plenty of poi, taro and fish and no want for anything like many a man at home." Such was the answer of a person who had been in England with their king, and who, on the passage back to their own country, had been fed by Lord Byron in a style not inferior to what he usually did himself.

June 10. 7 a.m. Saw Mouna Kaah far above the clouds, in places covered with snow. Fine appearance. Light rain after dark.

[44]Manuia.

June 11. Fine strong E. breezes. Mouna Roa, with its round flat top in sight, bearing South, and Mouna Kaah N.E., as also the high land of Mowee about N. During the day, several showers, fresh breezes and cloudy at 7 p.m.

ARRIVES AT HILO. PREPARES FOR ASCENT OF MAUNA KEA.

June 12. Sunday. Strong E.N.E. breezes and cloudy. At 10 a.m., church service, the queens, chiefs and missionaries present. Shortened sail and came to anchor in 6 fathoms. I got Lord Byron to gain Queen Kaumanna's consent for me to have 7 or 8 natives to accompany me to Mouna Kaah. After her usual "hesitation to consider," she said I might have as many as I wanted. I also asked her for a hut on shore to which to remove my traps tomorrow, where Mr. Forder will live till I return and where he can dry what plants I may find necessary to send home while on my journey. She desired that I should be informed that she did not know of a hut, but when she went on shore she would enquire of the chiefs.

REV. MR. GOODRICH, MISSIONARY

June 13. Went on shore to find the huts of the only two foreigners at this place, besides the missionaries, to procure one of these men as a guide to Mouna Kaah. I met Mr. Goodrich, one of the missionaries from Woahoo, who told me that both of the persons of whom I was in search had left the place a fortnight ago, to kill wild cattle near Mouna Kaah, and would probably not return for some weeks. He said that rather than I should be disappointed, he would willingly accompany me. His kind offer I accepted.

It was thought best to go the first part of the journey by canoe, and so save 30 miles of travel over many deep ravines and large rivers. We might return by land if we wished. For this water plan we had again to apply, through Lord Byron, to Queen Kaumanna for a canoe and also extra natives to man it. This Lord Byron, in his usual pleasant manner, promised to do when he found her (Queen Kaumanna) in such humour as likely not to refuse him, she at present being rather sulky from accounts received of some persons on shore having acted wrongly in her absence.

Lord Byron gave Mr. Talbot, fourth lieutenant, and Mr. Wilson, purser, permission to accompany me on my journey, and also acquainted me that Queen Kaumanna had promised me the canoe and natives for the next day. At noon I went on shore to choose a suitable hut, and met Mr. Goodrich, who went with me to look at the huts round the bay, all pleasantly situated under the shade of breadfruit trees, which in places form woods by themselves, and grow to a great height, producing plenty of fruit, although they possess but little variety and are generally of the small kind. There are here also plenty of both kinds of rose apple and coconut trees, some of the latter being of great height and age.

Heddo Bay and its neighbourhood are very pleasant on account of its woody appearance and plentiful supply of water, and is far superior in scenery to any spot we had seen either at Mowee or Woahoo, but like these is little cultivated, and only round about the native huts with patches of bananas, taro, tapa plants, etc. At the west end of the bay is a fair sized river with several waterfalls, convenient for watering ships, and in the centre of the bay is another subterranean one, which is dammed up a little distance from the sea and forms a large fresh water fish pond, tabooed for the use of the king and the chiefs. Toward the east end, not far from the shore and near a reef which runs partly across the bay, there is a small island thickly covered with low coco-nut trees, from which circumstance it is called Coco-nut Island.

The whole of the E. side of Owhyee, which is divided into two districts, belongs to Kaumanna and Pio. When at Heddo, their place of residence to receive the rents, is near the east side of the bay, and consists of no more than two huts, one of which is given to Lord Byron as a residence while here.

Returning on board, I heard that the canoe and natives would not be ready until tomorrow. Mr. Young this evening gave me some account of Mr. Menzies' journey to Mouna Roah,[45] next highest to Mouna Keah to which I am going. During the 26 years that Mr. Young has been on the island, he has never seen Mouna Kaah free from snow, but has not seen snow on Mouna Roah in summer, and on this he bases his theory of the greater height of Mouna Kaah.

[45]Archibald Menzies, a Scottish surgeon and naturalist, was the first white man to ascend to the top of Hualalai and the first white man and probably the first human being to reach the summit of Mauna Loa. For an account of his trips up these mountains, see "Hawaii Nei 128 Years ago," Honolulu 1920.

June 14. Went on shore with my traps, taking Mantle and
another lad Trounce with me. They both belonged to the ship,
and are allowed to me as long as I need them. I found that
the hut promised me by Manaware was now refused, and only
part of another offered, at the other side of the bay, and inhabited by a chief. My traps and provisions now being landed on
the beach and surrounded by crowds of natives who would not
have hesitated to make free with what they could lay hold of, I
begged to be allowed to put them in a corner of his Lordship's
house. Lord Byron told me it would make no difference to him
leaving any of my things there if I liked till I returned, but if I
wanted a place for them and Mr. Forder, I could have the tent
put up near his hut for his servants, and this I accepted.

I went with some of the missionaries to Queen Kaumanna's
hut to ask her whether I could depend upon the canoe for tomorrow. I found her, as usual, lying on the floor with her face
downwards, and several natives round her brushing the flies away
from her body. She hesitated in giving an answer until she had
surveyed me from head to foot, and then said when she saw one
of the chiefs, she would let me know. So I got Mr. Young, who
had more influence with her than the missionaries, to tell her I
would pay what money she wanted. This offer had the desired
effect, for she instantly sent across the bay to the head chief, and
when he came it was settled at once that I should have the canoe
and natives without paying at all. I sent word to Talbot and
Wilson to have everything ready on board for the morrow's start
when I came alongside in the canoe. I dined at 4 p.m. with Lord
Byron, the surgeon, chaplain and painter, who are his usual companions while on shore. Mr. Forder joined me at sunset, and we
took up our abode in Lord Byron's servants' tent.

START FOR MAUNA KEA

June 15. Fine day after a showery night during which the
rain poured through the old tent. Mr. Goodrich arrived at daylight with the double canoe and natives, and we immediately began to embark our provisions, etc., for our journey. It was 6
o'clock, however, before we got alongside the ship, for Messrs.
Talbot and Wilson, who were ready waiting for us. There were
now 17 on board the canoe, eleven natives and six of ourselves.
We started with the well wishes of all on board the Blonde for

our journey of 30 miles to Lapahoi[46] on the W. side of the island.

Favourable light east breezes, which freshened every hour until we landed in a narrow creek at 11 o'clock a.m. The creek was full of rocks, and open to a high surf that is generally found on this coast, and which at all times, except early in the morning, makes landing very difficult and dangerous, as we ourselves experienced. We had the greatest difficulty to prevent our canoe from being dashed on shore, owing to the surf washing over us every minute and filling the canoe with water so fast as to render our efforts in baling it out useless. We got into dry clothes as far as possible and dried our firearms, and then found that the 40 lbs. of salt meat which I had for my share of the provisions was missing, but nothing else.

LAUPAHOEHOE

Lapahoi is a small stony flat with a few huts and sweet potatoes and taro patches scattered over it. It lies at the extremity of a deep ravine, the declivities on either side nearly 500 feet in height and extending to the sea beach, terminating in a rocky precipice. The coast all the way to Lapahoi was intersected by many deep ravines, many of which had large rivers forming beautiful waterfalls that fell over the outward cliffs into the ocean, the angry surf of which broke a long way up upon the rocks underneath.

On the upper part of the inclines a species of pandanus grew plentifully. It is commonly used by the natives for making mats for the floors of their huts. It forms thick plantations here, giving the coast a pleasant appearance with their green bushy tops hanging pendant over the rocks where underneath in many places small subterranean streams fall down at no great distance from each other. This species of pandanus is nowhere so plentiful in the Sandwich Islands as on the island of Owhyee. It is cultivated elsewhere frequently for its leaves for mats and pillows for the natives. The tea tree is also plentiful here in the valleys along the coast.

CLIMBING MAUNA KEA

By noon we had finished taking some refreshments and dividing our baggage into loads for the natives to carry. We

[46]Laupahoehoe.

RUINS OF JOHN YOUNG'S HOUSE, KAWAIHAE, HAWAII

proceeded on our journey, leaving behind us six natives with orders to remain four days with the canoe in case we might return in that time and select to go home by water. The other five we took with us, making with ourselves eleven. On the summit above Lapahoi, we stopped to draw breath, and then every step became more interesting as we followed the narrow path to the woods above, which were yet four miles away. As we went along, the few native huts on either side were fast disappearing. The whole face of the country from the coast to six miles inland produced various fine prospects which reminded us of home, and if only cultivated, would produce an equal return of crops to any land of similar climate. But it is not even pastured by live stock, being covered with long grass and short stumpy tree ferns belonging to the Cyathea tribe, whose roots afford food for the swine about the huts of the natives.

These same huts are often inhabited by four generations, huddled together at night time like so many dumb animals, and often without sufficient shelter over them to protect them from the cold heavy dews that invariably fall here at night. We reached the outskirts of the woods between three and four in the afternoon, having on our way crossed three narrow deep ravines, thickly covered with wood, mostly *metrosideros, aleurites,* and a species of *rhus,* but without water except during heavy rains.

Our guide (Mr. Goodrich) recommended us to take up our quarters in these huts for the night, as these were the last inhabited ones on our way to the mountain where we had any chance to procure food to eat now and also to take with us, which on account of our loss on landing in the surf, we should now need. When about to enter the largest of the huts to prospect its condition, Mr. Goodrich was accosted by a smiling young woman, the wife of one of those Europeans who had come to kill wild cattle. She informed us that she had only left the Europeans yesterday morning, and that they had shot two bullocks the day before. We went and took possession of the cleanest part of the hut for our accommodation, without leave, as is customary with these people themselves, while Mr. Goodrich went in search of a young pig or fowls. All that he could procure, in spite of offering money and looking glasses, were a couple of fowls, owing to the price put upon their pigs, being nearly treble their worth.

Mr. Wilson was found in the midst of a crowd of natives, highly amused and viewing them with surprise. I went to the wood, while supper was being prepared, to look for plants, and found several species of ferns not seen before, and a few plants. I only got as far as the outskirts of the wood and the trees, which were of moderate size, consisted mostly of metrosideros and aleurites, with many ferns growing beneath their shade. In addition to the different species of metrosideros in variety of colours of the flowers as well as foliage already met with at Woahoo, there still appears in this island many which will add to their number, one particularly with straw-coloured flowers and white underneath the leaves, met with this evening, although sparingly, adds to my former collection.

When I got back, I found my three fellow travellers sitting on a mat, each holding a piece of fowl in one hand a clasp knife in the other, busy eating in the presence of a number of natives, some of whom had in their hands a light made from the kernels of the kukui or candle nut tree (*aleurites*) several nuts being passed through on a splinter of bamboo cane which gave a greater light than two or three common sized candles.

At 9 p.m. we retired to rest in a corner of the hut on a clean mat brought with us for the purpose, the rest of the hut being filled with the usual medley of men, women, children and dogs.

June 16. Fine but somewhat foggy. Got up at daylight, took the temperature of the air, which stood at 64. We were all ready to start at 5 a.m. in spite of the heavy dew which was still on the grass and bushes, and we were soon wet through by it up to our knees. We entered the wood about a mile from the edge of a small ravine, by a narrow path, where on either side grew a number of strong, healthy banana trees without cultivation and many of them having large bunches of fruit.

JOHN YOUNG AND ISAAC DAVIS'S FIRST BATTLE

Mr. Goodrich informed us that it was at this ravine that Mr. Young and Mr. Davis had fought their first battle in the service of Tamahamaah and defeated upwards of 10,000 of the enemy with only 300 on their own side, before their leader came up to their assistance with the main body of the army. The description related to us of this engagement was that when King Tamahamaah had conquered the south side of Owhyee, he soon after, with his army, marched round to the opposite side of the island by the east, taking with him Young and Davis for the first time, to whom he gave command of the chief part of his army. The chief of the Heddo part of the island was prepared to meet Tamahamaah in order to defend his proportion of the island from being subjected to the other's power, but on seeing the superior force of Tamahamaah, this chief kept retreating to the west till overtaken by Young and Davis, who were nearly a day's journey in advance of the main body of the army. The attack took place early in the afternoon from the opposite sides of the ravine in the wood, when after several hours engagement, it was decided in favor of Young and Davis, who alone had firearms. These two killed the enemy in vast numbers from the crowded manner in which they stood to oppose them, being unacquainted with the destructive effects of firearms.

This battle gave Tamahamaah the conquest of Owhyee.

We halted at 9 a.m. for refreshment, having travelled four miles through the wood, and I had the opportunity to ramble a little out of the path while the others rested. The trees now became more lofty, particularly a species of acacia used by the natives for canoes. Ferns of all kinds and sizes covered the ground beneath the trees, and a good many grew as parasites on the tree trunks. A noble species of Cyathea, equally numerous with the rest, often attained the height of 25 feet. Metrosideros with red bunchy flowering tops, covered with many red birds sucking their blossoms, were here much larger and taller than any seen on Woahoo. Besterias of various coloured flowers, and some of a climbing nature, and a numerous tribe of Psychotrias, both shrubby and succulent, as also many lobelias and other plants, aided by their variety to enliven our journey in spite of the many difficulties encountered from trees fallen across the path every other short distance, that had to be scrambled over. The path being slippery from the night rains occasioned many falls.

WILD RASPBERRIES AND STRAWBERRIES PLENTIFUL

After travelling another nine miles, we halted to fill our calabashes, this being the last place where we could obtain water till our return from Mouna Kaah. Here again, I took the temperature of the air. It had risen to 69. Towards the end of the wood the path became steeper. Here we found raspberries and strawberries of various kinds covered with fruit which we all ate eagerly to quench our thirst. The raspberries were very large and flat at both ends, but round in the middle and not unpleasant in flavour. The strawberries were small and great quantities of fruit grew around us on every side and looked like a neglected garden.

BULLOCK HUNTERS

We reached the end of the wood by 1 p.m., having travelled twelve miles, and above 12,000 feet above sea level. Here we found the two Europeans' temporary hut. They had been killing some of the wild cattle that had originally been introduced by Capt. Vancouver from the N.W. Coast of America and since suffered to remain unmolested for over 20 years. Since the death of King Tamahamaah the government has killed and salted many of the cattle for the supply of its small fleet. In the hut we found both the Europeans at home, asleep, and dressed in the costume of the country. There were also twenty natives, men, women and children outside, some asleep and others roasting pieces of flesh on a stick stuck in the ground slanting over the fire. Both the white men were well known to our guide, and being told of the object of our visit, offered to supply us with what beef we wanted. While the natives were cooking food for us we learned from these two half-naked foreigners, who could speak but little English, although one was a Welshman and the other a Prussian black-smith, and both for some time had been in the English navy, that they had succeeded in shooting several cattle, but with some difficulty, for the cattle often in droves of twenty were always sensible of any person approaching them. If unsuccessful in killing them with the first shot, it was absolutely necessary to have a place of retreat for their own safety, as they invariably pursued their destroyers with a kind of furious madness while they appear in sight.

Two days before, they had killed an old black bull, which they thought was one of the original number brought from California by Vancouver, from part of the right ear being cut off for a mark. They had been told that this had been put upon the cattle when landed thirty years ago. They have now increased to some hundreds, but it is curious that they have never been seen more than a few miles downwards in the wood from the mountain, and then only in warm weather for the sake of shade and water. Neither has a young one ever been got hold of and domesticated, although often attempted, for the mother living with her young, always seeks some retired place till the young ones are old enough to protect themselves.

I placed all the specimens I had collected since the commencement of our journey, in paper to be left till my return, and then went into the wood to look for more. Took the temperature of the air at 3 p.m., and found it was at 69, being the same as at 10 a.m. coming through the wood. Our guide told us we must travel at least 6 miles further towards the mountain to be able to gain the summit at an early hour tomorrow, before the horizon rose to prevent us from seeing the ship at anchor in the harbour. So waking my sleeping companions, we started on our next stage. However, a native unfortunately dropped a calabash of strong brandy and water (two gallons) being the last of my share of the spirits brought on the journey. We had scarcely travelled three miles when a thick fog commenced to roll in over the country which was covered with tufts of dry grass and full of cattle tracks. The soil was chiefly composed of sandy, pulverized lava, with numerous beds of strawberries growing on same. Raspberries grew in great abundance by the sides of the small ravines made by the torrents of water from the melted snow running here at certain seasons. They were of a better flavour than those in the upper part of the wood, being here more exposed to the sun.

By 6 p.m. we had travelled another two miles, when the fog became so thick that we were scarcely able to see ten yards ahead of us, and we were drenched and shivering with cold and almost beyond any vegetation to shelter us for the night. So we cut down boughs of Acacia and a species of Sophora and erected a hut. This we accomplished in little more than half an hour, and getting plenty of firewood kept a fire burning all night near where we lay. I rambled about till dark among cranberry bushes cutting specimens. The temperature at 7 p.m. was 52.

TOO COLD FOR NATIVES

Got up at 2 a.m., started at 3 and began our journey to the mountains leaving the natives behind, who feared the cold and did not want to accompany us. At 5 a.m., daylight began to appear and by then we had travelled three miles over sandy pulverized lava, sinking over our ankles at every step.

THE SILVER SWORD PLANT

The last mile was destitute of vegetation except one plant of the Syginesia tribe, in growth much like a Yucca, with sharp pointed silver coloured leaves and green upright spike of three or four feet producing pendulous branches with brown flowers, truly superb, and almost worth the journey of coming here to see it on purpose.[47] The majestic clouds rising on the horizon at day-break encircled us all round like an immense wall with towers of various forms and sizes on their tops. They lay at unequal distances along the horizon, gradually rising and changing into fresh shapes at every moment that had the finest effect imaginable.

TALBOT AND WILSON UNABLE TO PROCEED

The temperature had now fallen to freezing point. Messrs. Talbot and Wilson, overcome by the cold, became so sleepy as to be unable to proceed. We waited by them for some time trying to rouse them without avail, so leaving one of the lads with them, my guide and I with the other lad started out afresh so as to reach the summit and see the ship, we having promised Lord Byron to light a fire that he might see through his glasses how far we had got. As we advanced, every step became steeper and more difficult. All vegetation had ceased , even the yucca-looking plant, but we got up the mountain by 6 a.m., and saw the ship looking to us down there like a 50-ton vessel. Here we collected enough stumps and leaves to light a fire, remaining by it for half an hour, and our companions not overtaking us, we kept on our way, at times over hard uneven lava, at others over sandy lava.

REACHES MAIN PLATEAU OF MAUNA KEA

The mountain now became divided into several high conical sandy hills with several old small volcanic craters on their sides, forced above the sand for some yards in height and bleached nearly white from long exposure. The air became warmer and more pleasant as the sun rose above the horizon, but we had

[47]The Silver Sword plant of Hawaii was first brought to the knowledge of the botanical world by Dr. W. J. Hooker, who described it from specimens collected by David Douglas when he ascended Mauna Kea in 1834. See "David Douglas, Botanist at Hawaii," Honolulu 1919. Macrae climbed Mauna Kea in 1825, i.e., nine years ahead of Douglas, and must be credited with having been the first botanist to notice and collect the silver sword plant. Some modern writers persist in stating that the silver sword plant is found on Maui only. This is not the case, as it also grows on the high mountains of Hawaii.

constantly to rest from the difficulty of breathing after stopping to rest. At 8 a.m. we saw the lad, left with Talbot and Wilson, coming after us. Thinking he might have a message from them, we waited, but he had left the others still asleep, and only came to beg to be allowed to return, as he had been so cold waiting by the sleeping men. Giving him some refreshment and spirits, we sent him back to try and meet Talbot and Wilson. The temperature had now risen to 46, the sun shining brightly. We resumed our journey by the bottom of the sandy conical hills, the surface over which we travelled constantly changing and more uneven, sometimes being lava sand intermixed wtih small broken stones about the size of brickbats, and at other places having to scramble over large sharp-edged granite stones of several tons weight, which have beyond a doubt, been thrown up by some previous convulsion. We came in sight of the snow after 11 a.m. Our guide seemed to suffer more than the lad and myself from headache and inclination to vomit, and we had yet two miles to go over a still more rugged surface to reach the snow.

MR. GOODRICH COLLAPSES

At a quarter mile from the summit where the snow lay, our guide collapsed and begged us to get him some snow for his thirst.[48] The lad Mantle held out better than I had expected.

MACRAE AND BOY MANTLE REACH SUMMIT

At 12.30 I reached the snow on the summit, which lay on porous lava of a sponge color, and in places on sand of a red color intermixed with red and black cinders like the conical hills we had passed. Some of these cinders had common quartz and two or

[48]Rev. Joseph Goodrich, who, on this occasion, was unfortunately laid up with mountain sickness, had on 26th August, 1823, reached the summit of Mauna Kea. This is the first recorded instance of the ascent of this mountain, although Mr. Goodrich mentions that on reaching the top of one of the terminal cones that encircle the main plateau of Mauna Kea, he discovered a heap of stones, probably erected by some former visitor. Who this former visitor was is unknown, but he was probably one of the white men that in the early years of the nineteenth century got a living by shooting wild bullocks that roved on the side of Maunt Kea. It is very unlikely that any native had reached the top of the terminal cones on the summit, owing to being unprovided with warm clothing to resist the great cold and also to the fact that the natives had a superstitious dread of the mountain spirits or gods. About six months after the date of the first ascent of Mauna Kea by Mr. Goodrich, the peak was scaled by Dr. Abraham Blatchley and Mr. Samuel Ruggles, both connected with the American Mission.

three other kinds of minerals that I am as yet unacquainted with, very often bedded in one lump of lava. The snow in some parts was about three feet deep, congealed into solid ice, excepting from two to three inches at top of rough particles of loose snow. The whole appeared to be melting fast through the porous lava like a sieve, which prevented our being able to fill our vessels with water. We therefore filled our handkerchiefs with snow, taking mouthfuls at the same time to quench our thirst. I sent Mantle with some snow to our guide, and remained to take the temperature in the sun and in the shade. In the former it was 92, and in the latter, in holes beneath the snow, 44. I stayed about an hour admiring the scenery. For a space of about 12 miles around the top of the mountain, it was dreary to a degree, but below that, the pasture where the wild cattle fed had a pleasing effect. The forest which encircles the island of Owhyee below the pasture land, was hidden in fog, so that I only saw about 20 miles in a direct line, but the high land like Mouna Roa and other hills could be easily distinguished above the fog, although none of them were covered with snow.

SHEEP KILLED OFF BY WILD DOGS

I saw many skeletons of some kind of animal, devoid of all flesh, but apparently not long dead, and on rejoining our guide, was informed that the wild dogs had almost exterminated the sheep that Vancouver had brought with the cattle, pursuing them beyond the line of vegetation, where they became bewildered and died for want of food.

BEGINS RETURN JOURNEY

It being now after 2 p.m., and still feeling unwell from the same causes as our guide, we left this interesting place and travelled slowly downwards, finding our few specimens of minerals, etc., almost twice their real weight. In this hobbling manner, scarcely able to drag our limbs for the last four miles, we reached our hut, where we found that the lad sent back in the morning to Messrs. Talbot and Wilson had not met them. So fearing they might have succumbed to the cold in their sleep, and knowing they had no provisions, we much repented having left them; but to our joy, in about half an hour, we heard them calling not far distant. When they came to the hut they did not appear so fatigued as we ourselves, in spite of the want of food. They had slept for about an hour, then awoke and tried to follow us, but not finding any of our tracks, they gave up the idea of following us, and made for the first of the highest hills. The snow we had brought with us served us well with water, for the natives left behind had drunk all that we left of the latter article except about a pint. The natives rubbed our thighs and legs for us, a practice they often do for themselves in such circumstances. They call it lummi lummi. The temperature at 7 p.m. was 50 and at 10 p.m. 48.

We calculated the summit of Mouna Kaah from Byron's (or Heddo) Bay to be about 70 miles by the common path, but in a direct line perhaps only half that distance. We judged the peak could not be under 18,000 feet above sea level.[49] The land along the sea coast from Byron's Bay to upwards of 40 miles to the west and about 6 miles in breadth, was free from wood excepting by the sides and bottoms of the ravines. The forest that surrounds the central part of the island begins here, at the distance of 5 or 6 miles from the coast, and stretches back for a depth of 12 miles, intersected with deep valleys and large rivers of fine water. The outskirts of the forest nearest the sea are chiefly handsome coloured flowering species which entirely disappear after 5 or 6 miles towards the centre of the wood. The commonest species of metrosideros often attains a height of 40 feet and are thick in proportion. The wood is hard and durable.

The upper parts above the forest resemble pasture land for 7 miles farther, and are thinly covered with low growing shrubs and abundance of strawberries and raspberries. At a higher elevation, vegetation ceases for the last eight miles towards the summit. The clouds generally rise on the mountains of Owhyee and the other islands in the morning and disperse towards evening. Rain often falls at night and also in the daytime some distance from the peaks, while on the coast the sun may be shining and there is no appearance of rain.

June 18. Got up at daylight, being disturbed in the night by the howling of wild dogs which caused us to keep our fire burning. At six set out on our homeward way, and unknown to us, the natives at once set fire to our discarded hut, a common custom our guide told us. At 12 we had travelled 6 miles and reached the Prussian and Welshman's hut. These men had seen no wild cattle since we left them, the only animals observed having been

[49]Mauna Kea is 13,825 feet high.

a wild dog and cat. The dog seemed to be the same kind as the domesticated native one of which they eat the flesh, and the cat appeared like the European breed. After a breakfast of plenty of slices of roast beef and abundance of water, my companions spread their mats in the shade and slept till noon. I shifted my specimens that had been left here into dry papers, and gathered others, including strawberry and raspberry plants to take with me to England. At 2 the whole camp was on the move for Lapahoi, where we had left the canoe and the natives. On reaching the first hut, we found only the two foreigners, the rest having gone on to Lapahoi. They promised to have a fire ready for us to dry our clothes at, but although I gave them each a dollar on starting they had nothing ready for us and did not get us any food till 9 p.m.

NATIVES OBJECT TO SUNDAY TRAVEL

June 19. Hazy, light showers. Sunday, and on that account the natives refused to accompany me to join the other part of my party with their loads, and said the missionaries had ordered them not to.

GAME OF NOA

The blacksmith, however, promised to accompany me with his own people at 11 a.m., but instead of doing so, went and played and gambled at Nooah. This game is one of their most ancient and frequently played pastimes. It consists in placing in a row, five small tapa bags stuffed with cotton or the down of ferns, underneath one of which is hidden a stone so as to deceive the parties playing which of the bags it was put under. The players are seated around in a circle, each armed with a small wand in his hand with which he strikes the bag he supposes the stone to be under. There are generally ten players with different coloured rags tied to their wands. I have been told that at this game they gamble their hogs and all their possessions, even their wives, and are very strict in paying their debts of honor.

Leaving them gambling, I left with the two lads and two natives for Lapahoi, and joined my party there about 3 p.m. They were just about to start for home, having expected me in the morning. The canoe had not waited for us as ordered but had returned home the second day after we started for the mountain. We therefore had to go home by land, and took up our quarters for the night about 7 p.m. after having crossed a number of deep ravines, wading through rivers, at times up to our middle.

Having travelled about 10 miles east of Lapahoi, the natives lighted a fire, for we were drenched, and cooked some bananas and breadfruit. To do this, they first of all got some stones heated red hot, then afterwards put them into a gourd calabash with a few leaves of the tea tree underneath and the same again above. Then were added cabbages cut in pieces, intermixed with bananas that had only the outer skin taken off. Over all on top were put more leaves to prevent the steam rising upwards. In about a quarter of an hour the mess was ready to eat, and our vegetable supper was by no means unpalatable.

DIFFICULT TRAVELLING OVER RAVINES

June 20. Cloudy and cold. Got up at 4 a.m., and commenced our journey of crossing ravines and fording rivers, taking off our shoes for surer footing. At one river Mr. Talbot nearly came to grief, for insisting on crossing at the same place as the natives, in spite of their protests that he did not know, as they did, where to find the stones on which to place his feet, after a few steps he was swept off his feet, and managed to get hold of a stone that was above the water whereon happened to stand two natives, who caught hold of his hands, but a third native attempting to lay hold of his body was carried away by the current to some distance not far off from a waterfall. The natives holding Talbot could not drag him out, for one of his legs was caught between two stones. I saw the whole affair but could not get to him, having waited to go higher up to a surer place with Wilson, but I managed to get near enough to get the barrel of my gun under his leg and succeeded in extricating it, after which the natives were able to pull him out of the water.

The natives had shown great anxiety to get Talbot out of danger, and as a mark of gratitude, he gave them each a knife. He was little the worse except for bruises. The natives said that if he had been drowned, Kaumanna would have been sure to have killed them for not saving his life. All the rest got safely across, but we soon came to another river as large, and at this one Mr. Wilson fell and broke our flask with the little remains of our brandy! At 9 a.m. we halted at a large hut and breakfasted off a few taros and some poi. Then continuing on our way we crossed ravines 400 to 500 feet deep with fine, clear water at the bottom. The sides of these ravines had plenty of rose apple, breadfruit trees, pandanus, ferns and other plants.

GETS BACK TO HILO

We arrived opposite the ship at 5 p.m. very tired from our many climbs up and down, since we left Lapahoi on Sunday, distant 40 miles.

Mantle who had gone with me to the snow and two of the natives were the only three who had managed to keep up with us all the way. On getting on board the ship, where I was invited to dine with Talbot and Wilson, I heard that Mr. Forder was still with my things in the old tent, so I slipped away, got into a canoe again without dining, to find out why the things had never been moved according to promise.

June 21. Got my specimens into dry paper. The lad Trounce arrived saying he and my things had been upset out of the canoe in crossing the river at the watering place, but as he had nearly been drowned, I could not be angry, so again I had at once to set to work to shift everything into dry paper. Accompanied by Mr. Young, as interpreter, I succeeded in hiring a hut for the remainder of my stay, for which, in preference to money, I gave two blankets for three weeks.

NATIVE RENT COLLECTION

June 22. In the forenoon, over two hundred natives came from the east part of the island with their rents for Queen Kaumanna, such as tapa cloths,[50] and mats of various dyed patterns, hogs, taro, etc., etc. She never attempted to smile or give a pleasant look at the natives who brought this rent, although I heard she had not been on the island during the last four years.

[50] Down to about the end of the fifties of last century, the natives on the island of Oahu were in the habit of paying at least a share of their taxes in the form of tapas. The tapas were deposited in the Pa-auhau or tax yard, situated about where Marin Street is, near the foot of Nuuanu St., and west of Merchant Street. Messrs. Robinson and Lawrence had a ship repairing yard at "the point," near where the fort stood. They were in the habit of buying these tapas from the government and used them for felt under the sheets of copper nailed on the sides of vessels that were being repaired. Tapa or kapa making is now a thing of the past in Hawaii, but the process of making it may still be seen in Fiji, Tonga, and Samoa. In the Cook group, Tahiti and other South Sea islands, tapa has given place to gaudy colored cotton prints, woven in Manchester and dyed in Glasgow.

I asked her permission, however, and she gave me three of the largest sugar canes as specimens. A mat which was given to the surgeon, I was informed, would take a woman a year to make. When the women get to a certain age, it is their duty to manufacture all the tapa cloths and mats.

On going to my hired hut to take my traps, and offering my two blankets, they did not want to let me have it after all, and the wife and some others shed tears. He told me it was their fear of my burning the hut when I went away, as was their custom. Being assured that I had no such intentions, they at once received me as tenant.

MACRAE'S HUT TABOOED

The chief man of the place came at Mr. Young's request to taboo my hut, to prevent my being crowded by the natives.

The charm was done thus: The chief stuck in the ground a few wands at some distance from each other, all round the hut, which on being seen by the natives, they never dare enter, unless sent with some message by any of the chiefs.

BOTANIZES IN PUNA

June 23. Went about nine miles east of Byron's Bay to collect plants, but met with little success. Messrs. Talbot and Wilson called to say they were going to the volcano on the 25th, and had come to make arrangements as to a guide and provisions to take with us.

JOURNEY TO KILAUEA VOLCANO

June 24. Arranged with the blacksmtih, met at Mouna Kaah, and five natives, to act as guide and carriers. The former recommended me to speak to Kaumanna in order to get her to order the latter not to leave us till our return.

June 25. Talbot and Wilson and the guide appeared, but none of the natives, so the guide had to go in search of them. By 7 a.m. the guide came back with the natives, and we began our journey as the first party for the volcano from the ship. His Lordship and several others intend to follow us in a few days. We travelled thirteen miles by 1 p.m., five miles of that distance being through a wood over a narrow path of broken pieces of sharp edged lava, which we could hardly bear our own weight upon without pain to our feet. This wood had many trees, mostly metrosideros of over 40 feet, but slender in proportion, and far inferior in size to those we met on our way to Mouna Kaah. Under their shade grow numbers of ferns which hide the lava.

At 6 p.m., having travelled 20 miles since leaving the ship, we reached a hut newly put up for the use of Lord Byron when he passes this way. The last six miles were through an open country, over solid greyish black undulated lava, covered with stumpy ferns, chiefly cythea, which the natives often burn during the dry season. We found also quantities of three sorts of cranberries on each side of the path. They were ripe and we enjoyed them much although somewhat acid. The road through which we had come, continued all the way up towards Mouna Roa.

We were joined in the hut for the night by numbers of natives, who without the slightest compunction, examined the skin of our hands and feet to see if it were the same colour as our faces. But a look from us would make the children under ten take to their heels. The old women generally nursed the children, carrying them on their backs, never in their arms. When travelling any distance, they tie the children to their back with a bandage of tapa cloth placed round the child's neck and thighs, so as to leave the woman's hands at liberty.

June 26. Wet and foggy, so could not resume our journey till after 8 a.m. Reached the last native huts on the way to the volcano by 12, having travelled 10 miles over the same kind of undulating lava as yesterday. Our guide here spent two hours trying to procure some fowls or a hog to take with us, but the natives wouldn't part with them unless we gave three times their value, so we started again with what little provision we had of our own with us. Our natives grumbled, saying they would have to eat ferns before they got back. However, after we had left the huts some distance, the natives who lived there sent after us a couple of fowls for which they would take no payment.

By 6 p.m. we reached two old hovels on the outskirts of the wood of acacia trees, having travelled about 18 miles since morning over lava covered with ferns, cranberries and low straggling bushes of red flowering metrosideros and along the last two miles, beds of strawberries growing under the ferns and grass on sandy pulverized lava. Here we stopped for the night, our guide saying we were not far from the volcano. Repaired the hovels, the natives making a fire to cook the fowls. Our guide reported he had seen the volcano smoking in the distance, but we hardly believed him.

KILAUEA IKI

June 27. Misty and foggy morning, so could not start till 7 a.m., when we passed on our left a large old volcano crater, over 1000 feet deep, now covered with verdure on its internal declivities, and the bottom, which is level, having a few low growing red flowering metrosideros bushes.

ARRIVES AT KILAUEA VOLCANO

At 8 a.m. we reached a shed in good condition, situated on the edge of the active volcano, which we now find we could easily have reached last night instead of staying and repairing the hovels. Besides we could have had the gratification of watching the burning craters during the night. Here we stood gazing on the immense depth below covered with clouds of smoke, while at short intervals a terrific noise was distinctly heard among the different burning craters.

DESCENDS INTO THE KILAUEA VOLCANO PIT

In the meantime the natives were busy making sandals of grass to protect their feet from the lava when they got below. At 8.30 we all eagerly began to descend from the hut, with walking sticks, there being nothing to hold by but short tufts of dry grass. The loose stones kept rolling amongst us all the way down to the first ledge, which we reached at 9.30, without any injury beyond bruises from the stones. The vegetation ceased at this point, the burning craters being at least 500 feet below us. Our road became more difficult and steep, over large irregular sharp-edged stones torn from their bed, piled up loose upon each other and intermixed with flat pieces of honey-combed lava.

By noon, with difficulty and danger, some of us had reached the nearest smoking pillar, about 30 feet high and covered with sulphur, which gave it a beautiful yellow appearance. We waited here some time for the natives to come up who had hurt their naked feet and legs in falling in through the hollow lava that lay in places resembling flues on the top of the more solid material underneath, which required the greatest caution to try it first with our sticks to see whether it would break before we attempted to advance a step upon it. We crossed many wide rents. Some

of these openings were constantly smoking and smelt so strong
of brimstone that got up our nostrils when going over them, as
nearly to suffocate us.

While standing by the brimstone pillar, we noticed that at
times there issued forth sudden gusts of smoke, strongly impreg-
nated with brimstone, which obliged us to be careful to avoid
when we approached near it for the purpose of picking up specimens of the hot lava covered with sulphur from the opening in
the sides. The natives who had experienced difficulty in coming thus far, besides fear, now begged leave to return again to
the top, which we readily granted, while we four went farther on
to examine another pillar about 50 feet high, burning red at the
top like a furnace and emitting to a considerable distance from it,
lumps of soft lava and cinders of various colours. On getting
near to the pillar, the terrific noise kept up underneath everywhere round it for a considerable way from where we stood, in-
timidated us that we were afraid that while we remained there,
the part underneath us might be torn to pieces every minute.

Frightful was the noise kept up by the burning beneath
among the numerous pillars, which were nearly hidden in smoke
and impossible of approach, except to windward, owing to the
strong smell of sulphur. The noise of the burning craters resembled a blacksmith's forge, and could be distinctly heard half
a mile away. At 1 p.m., as we had not time to stay longer, we
began to re-ascend at a point a mile farther to the north of the
hut from which we had started in the morning. We found the
temperature to be 92 in the shade, and in the sun it exceeded the
height of my thermometer, which was only marked up to 132.

The volcano is situated about 40 miles S.E. of Byron's Bay,
at the foot of Mouna Roa. According to the missionaries who
measured it some years ago, its circumference is 7 miles round
the edge at the top, and five miles round the almost circular basin
below. The depth is in most places from 1000 to 1200 feet. The
ledge, which is nearly perfect all round the basin is rather more
than half way down from the top. The number of burning
craters, in the form of pillars, exceeded twelve, some of which
were over 50 feet in height and generally of a bronze shining
colour and of various shapes, with several unequal openings on
their sides to the summit, where sudden gusts of smoke issue forth
at intervals.

Adjoining the craters where we had travelled, the surface varied. In some places the ground was covered with sharp-edged granite stones, piled up above each other, intermixed with similar hard stones of a red colour, or smooth and white, but in general the basin was composed of black and greyish porous honeycombed brittle lava, often undulated like waves of the sea, and where late convulsions had taken place, it formed at short distances hollow burning passages of great length, which are full of red and white ashes. When the thin crust above these passages are trod upon, it easily falls in. Most of the lava was crystallized in small particles on the top like glass, which if fallen upon, tore the skin of hands and feet through our clothes.

The internal declivities on the west side are steep and free from vegetation, but on the south and east sides vegetation continues in most parts to the first ledge and consists chiefly of the red flowering metrosideros, dwarfed in size, and mixed with tufts of two or three kinds of dry grasses. To the south we noticed a large space covered with brimstone, looking like the chalky cliffs of Dover and Gravesend. At 2 p.m. we gained the summit on the north side, where, near the top, I saw several bushes of sanders wood in flower, with a few other plants, but there were not the same variety as met with when nearly above the zone of vegetation on the slope of Mouna Kaah.

On the flat land at the top were several hot springs underneath narrow deep openings divided in the earth at short distances apart from each other, and spread over for half a mile in breadth from the edge of the volcano top, For more than a foot wide, these openings had on the surface of their sides, luxuriant patches of green moss growing from the moisture caused by the steam. Some of the water near the surface which we drank, was only warm. Here we noticed some sheds used by the natives when cutting trees for canoes. We also saw some remains of cooked fern (cythea) which our natives are glad to eat, and which we found not at all unpalatable.

We reached our previous night's resting place by 4 p.m., having met on our way with quantities of cranberries and strawberries. Some of the sulphur specimens which I had put in seed paper when down in the volcano at the first pillar, I found had already burnt through the paper and my coat pocket. Its taste was more acid than of sulphur. We then travelled homewards and reached the first huts soon after dark, and found waiting for us, the natives that we had allowed to return from the volcano. They had some taro and poi ready, being all the food they could obtain. Having mixed the poi with a little sugar brought by Talbot and Wilson for the purpose, and warming the taro before the fire, we managed to satisfy our hunger, and then retired to rest, hoping to get home the next morning.

MEETS LORD BYRON AND PARTY EN ROUTE TO VOLCANO

June 28. Got up at daylight and started for home. When we had gone four miles we met Lord Byron's party going to the volcano. It consisted of 30 natives with the head chief (Maro) at Byron's Bay as their leader, who had gone on ahead to have fires lighted to cook a meal for his Lordship. A little after these we met the naturalist and one of the missionaries, followed by the surgeon and draftsman, then the chaplain with two natives carrying his hammock slung to a pole, ready for him to get into when tired. Again after these came the surveyor, first lieutenant and another missionary and a boy middy. A short way in the rear was Lord Byron, accompanied by another middy who had his hammock with him ready to be carried like the chaplain. When we informed Lord Byron of our want of provisions, he told us to take anything we wanted from the carriers, as he had plenty of everything. We reached the hut where we had slept the first night at 8 p.m.

June 29. Sorted and packed up my specimens of lava.

NATIVE BURIAL CUSTOMS

June 30. A man about thirty years of age died in the evening, and I found his relatives had taken him out of his hut to breathe his last in a temporary shed, owing to a superstitious custom among them never to inhabit a hut where anyone had died, but to burn it immediately. The body was lying on a dirty mat rolled up in a piece of tapa cloth, with a few natives making a howling noise over it. On asking them what was the matter, they leaned their head on one hand, while they pointed the other towards the sky where they said he had gone to sleep and parted from them for ever. I told what I had seen to Mr. Young, saying I had never seen a funeral since I had been here. He replied that he had only seen one and that by a great favor. It took place

NUKU'IWI
"Iiwi's bill" (Strongylodon lucidum)

in the head of night, and was made up of a few old men and women who are always entrusted to bury the dead about that time with great secrecy, for what reasons he did not know, only supposed it to have arisen from an old superstitious custom. He said some of them never buried their dead, but concealed them for a certain time till the flesh decayed off the bones sufficiently dry to be tied up afterwards in a bundle of tapa cloth and then hung up inside the roof of their huts.

July 1. Lord Byron and his party returned from the volcano, some of them very lame.

VISITS WAIANUENUE OR RAINBOW FALLS

July 2. Went at 5 a.m. to see the waterfall above Byron's Bay, with Mr. Talbot and Mr. Goodrich, our Mouna Kaah guide. The fall was situated about six miles inland and was over 60 feet in height. The river is one of the largest on this side of the island, and like the rest has many falls upon it at no great distance from each other. I remained with Mantle in the wood till dusk, gathering plants, some of which I had not seen before, particularly a beautiful climbing plant, resembling an erythrina, with crimson flowers,[51] and several metrosideros and ferns. I learned on my return that Lord Byron intends to sail on Thursday, the 7th for certain, which prevents me from going again to collect in the woods.

July 3. Sunday. Fine. Busy all day among my specimens and seeds and writing. Another party of gentlemen from the ship have gone to the volcano to be back before the ship sails.

July 5. My last night on shore at Byron's Bay, as I have to be on the ship with all my traps by tomorrow morning.

July 6. At 4 a.m. a boat came and took me with all my belongings on board.

LEAVES HILO FOR OAHU

July 7. Weighed anchor at 5 a.m. and sailed for Woahoo taking with us the queens we had brought from thence, also two missionaries, their wives and families and over 100 natives. At 2 p.m. still light, variable winds, so lowered the boats to tow the ship off the land.

[51] Nukuiwi 'Strongylodon lucidum Seem.), i.e., Iiwi's bill or beak from the shape of the flower.

July 8. Fine, with fresh breezes from the east. Made Diamond point, near Hanarura at Woahoo. Stood off and on the land for the night.

HONOLULU ONCE MORE

July 9. Fine. Moderate breeze from the N.E. Came to anchor off the harbour of Hanarura. The pilot Adams came on board and reported that the Asia, 64, a Spanish ship, with two brigs in company, who were pirates on the coast of California, were said to intend touching here for supplies. This information came by a schooner lately arrived from the coast. In consequence, all was soon bustle to get the natives and their luggage on shore as soon as possible so that the guns might be mounted ready for action. At 9 a.m. Lord Byron requested me to go ashore and get my plant boxes on board at once, as he might get under weigh this evening and join the schooner at Karakaakua Bay. Went and returned with the boxes and found all the natives gone and the guns mounted and loaded, the sailors in high spirits, hoping for the enemy to give them battle and so gain a prize.

MARIN, THE SPANIARD

July 10. Sunday. Fresh N.E. wind. Went on shore as we were not to sail till tomorrow morning, not to return here again. I went to see what plants were left of those brought out from England. Met Lord Byron and Marin the Spaniard. We found only six plants and these without leaves. Marin said he had removed the others to his farm in the mountains, where many were doing well. To Mr. Marin's diligence as a farmer, the Sandwich Islands, particularly Woahoo, may be said to be under some obligations for his introducing and multiplying various kinds of animals, which in a few years will be plentiful on the island.

Tran^{co} de Paula i Marin

When I was about to leave Mr. Pitt, I requested the favour of Marin to inquire of him if he would give me some patterns of their native cloth for the Horticultural Society, and received for answer that he would consider of it. Remained on shore with

HONOLULU

(Looking towards Barber's Point)

Drawn by L. Choris

one of the gentlemen from the ship at the inn of Novara.

DUSTY HONOLULU

July 11. Fine, with strong wind, which raised clouds of dust in the town that nearly suffocated and blinded me. Since we had been at Owhyee, I found that Pitt, who was 60 years of age, had married a young woman of 19. She, with her sister, had lived with him for many years. This marriage is the second which has ever yet taken place in these islands. Went on board where all was in readiness to get under weigh when Lord Byron came on board.

July 12. Lord Byron on leaving the shore to embark, was saluted with 13 guns from the forts and was accompanied by Pitt, Boki and several other chiefs to take farewell of us. It was now understood on board that we were to leave the islands for Otahiti, after touching at Karakaakua Bay to take on board the surveyors out of the Sandwich Island schooner given them for their use by the government to survey on the coast. Pitt was most interested in examining everything on board, and requested Lord Byron to make all sail and get some distance to sea that he might see how we sailed. To humour him, Lord Byron had all the hands mustered and as they passed along in front of them they all saluted, to the scandal of some of the middies, etc., that British men-o-wars' men should salute a half-civilied savage, unaccustomed to such honour from his own bareheaded countrymen. At 3 p.m., made in again for the land sent them all on shore wtih a salute of 13 guns from the Blonde.

July 13. Fine, with moderate wind. Made sail as yesterday evening for Karakaakua Bay.

ANCHORS AT KEALAKEKUA BAY

July 14. Saw the high land of Owhyee, above the clouds, covered with snow. At 10 a.m. came to anchor at Karakaakua Bay in 26 fathoms. Went on shore and were shown where a cannon shot had gone through the trunk of a coconut tree, near where Capt. Cook was killed. Some of the others of our party went close to the water's edge looking at the spot where he fell. This place is at times overflown by the tide at high water. Having satisfied our curiosity here, we went to examine some caves close at hand in front of a steep volcanic rock which divides Karona from Karakaakua.[52] The first cave was full of dozens of old muskets apparently the manufacture of various countries. Scarcely one was complete. They were heaped up, broken in pieces and covered with rust. While hunting in the corner for curiosities, we found an old fishing rod (which was given to me) and a club. The rod was chiefly made of human bone, and the club made of wood shaped like a thigh bone. However, Lord Byron seeing the chief at his hut, prevented me from keeping the rod, as we had no permission to take anything away, so to our disappointment, it had to be replaced here we found it.

We next visited the spot where Captain Cook's body was said to have been divided by the chiefs.[53] It is about half a mile above Karona, on the top of a hill. We found the place had been held sacred for some time, judging from the appearance of the old lava walls raised round about 20 feet square and from 4 to 5 feet high, and nearly the same thickness.

In the evening we went across to the other side of the bay at Karakaakua, which, like Karona,[54] is composed of only a few straggling huts, under coconut trees growing entirely upon lava, without any signs of anything nutritious to support them. Near where the immortal Cook was cut up to be divided among the chiefs, grows a fine white flowering plant of a low shrubby nature not met with before in any other part.[55] It belongs to the tribe Diadelpha and is generally found only on the lava near to the sea coast, with scarcely any other vegetation near it. It had plenty of seeds which I gathered and am in hopes that it will grow in England.

July 15. Owing to the uncertainty as to our starting, I could only pick up the few plants growing on the barren fragments of

[52]Kaawaloa from Kealakekua.

[53]This spot is known to Hawaiians as "Kapuhiolono," "the burning of Lono," i.e., Captain Cook.

[54]Kaawaloa, or as it is generally pronounced Ka-ava-loa. There is a distinct "V" sound in some Hawaiian words, such as "Ewa," pronounced "Eva." Andrews in compiling his dictionary of the Hawaiian language, saw fit to ignore the "V" sound, as he has also that of "T," which is still to be heard on the island of Kauai or Tauai.

[55]Here is possibly meant Puapilo (Capparis sandwichiana D.C.).

black lava near the sea shore and for several miles inland. Beyond the fringe of bare lava, the ground gradually rises to the woody mountains that appear covered with cultivated patches of sweet potatoes, taro, breadfruit and banana trees.

The whole coast on this side of the island has a horrid and dreary appearance. The ground is everywhere covered with cinders and streaks and hollow parts which mark the course of lava from Mouna Roa. The natives have shown great industry in clearing away the top lava to the depth of 4 feet or so in order to get to the more fertile soil underneath, which is composed of rich ashes and a light mould. On Owhyee, the taro is little cultivated in ponds of water as at Woahoo and Mowee, and is consequently of much smaller growth but dry and farinaceous. The sea here, like at other parts of the islands we touched at, abounds with a variety of excellent fish of many colours. What little water is met with is generally brackish.

COOK'S OBSERVATORY

We saw at Karakaakua the large heap of stones where Capt. Cook had his observatory, which was formerly a morai and religious places for human sacrifices.[56] We also noticed near the same place three coconut trees with cannon shot holes through them from the firing upon the natives which took place when Capt. Cook was killed. In the gardens of the native huts grow a few tobacco plants and banana trees for immediate use. We saw a dog being cooked for one of the chiefs, who consider them better eating than any other animal.

VISITS THE PUUHONUA AT HONAUNAU AND HALE O KEAWE

July 16. Went to see the morai[57] on the other side of the island. On our way met the old priest in his canoe coming on board. He alone is entrusted to enter the morai, and we accordingly took him back with us. We found the morai was on the

[56]Hikiau heiau or temple.

[57]By morai is meant the Hale o Keawe. Although Macrae does not mention the large Puuhonua or City of Refuge, he must have visited it as it immediately adjoins the ground where the Hale o Keawe stood. For particulars about the Hale o Keawe, see article by Prof. W. D. Alexander in Vol. 3 of the Polynesian Society Journal. Dampier, the Blonde's artist, made a sketch of this building, which has often been republished.

east point of a small bay surrounded by huts standing under a thinly scattered grove of coconut trees, but with no signs of cultivation about.   As we were about to enter the morai the old priest, who had on a straw hat and cotton shirt, took both of them off, and only left his maro on.   On entering we only found an empty filthy hut with quantities of human bones in heaps under mats at each end of the hut, many of the bones not yet dry and disgusting to the sight.   In the middle were several effigies of the deceased chiefs, tied to a bundle of tapa cloth containing the bones of each person whom the effigies represented.   Most of the effigies were made of wood, but the one representing the late Tamahamaah was substituted by a mask of European manufacture and was more finely dressed than the others.   The party with Lord Byron that had visited here the day before, had taken away any memorials of the morai that could be taken, so we asked the old priest to be allowed to take some of the ancient weather beaten carved figures outside.

The morai is a small thatched hut fenced round with sticks to the height of 6 feet, kept together by two rows of bars. Fixed in the lava ground at the entrance front stand upright several various sized wooden rudely carved hideous figures, in representation of their former gods.   These they now set but little value upon, and are rarely met with in the huts of the natives.

We travelled home by land along the sea coast, over uneven masses of lava, and meeting with only a few plants such as tufts of low-growing euphorbias, convolvuluses, sidas, but mostly diadelphas plant seen common at the place where the chiefs shared between them the body of Capt. Cook.   There was also a species of hibiscus, with yellow flowers, much used here by the natives to dye their tapa cloths yellow.   On the way home, we passed a number of heaps of lava raised over the dead slain in one of Tamahamaah's battles for the conquest of the island. This was between the morai and Karakaakua.

On board we found the old priest awaiting us for some presents in return for the old images he had allowed us to take from outside the morai. We gave him several articles of clothing with which he was more pleased than if we had given him money.

VISITS KAPUHIOLONO AND ERECTS MONUMENT TO CAPTAIN COOK'S MEMORY

July 17. Sunday. Fine. Went to see the monument erected yesterday to the memory of Capt. Cook by his Lordship (Byron) on the top of the black lava hill above Karona, where it is said his body was divided amongst the chiefs. This monument is simply a capstan bar from the ship, painted white and fixed on a heap of lava that had formerly been raised by the natives when they made the square wall round this spot, which they now for years look upon as consecrated ground.

This bar stands about sixteen feet high, with a small copper plate at the top, having the following inscription upon it:
In memory of Captain James Cook, R.N.,
who discovered these islands
in the year of Our Lord 1778
This humble monument is erected by his fellow countrymen
in the year of Our Lord 1778

THE BLONDE SAILS FOR TAHITI

July 18. At 12.10 a.m. weighed anchor and made sail with light breezes for Otahite, leaving these interesting islands after a short stay of little more than two months. With the exception of a few chiefs of high rank, who have adopted a little of the European style of costume, the natives still retain their manners and customs nearly the same as related by the unfortunate Cook who fell a sacrifice to their barbarity. The dagger which is said to have committed the fatal deed, I am now informed, is in the possession of a gentleman on board, who is also informed of every particular circumstance relating to the misunderstanding which took place between the parties at the time. But I am inclined to doubt if they had such a thing as a dagger at that period, or why it should be held secret from Vancouver and other navigators who were equally anxious to gain all information respecting the occurrence and with what weapon the fatal deed was committed. The small English drum presented by Cook to the King is now in his Lordship's possession, with some other things which have been in the morai for many years and were given to Lord Byron when he visited the morai a few days ago.

(Here follows in Macrae's manuscript a list of 25 fruits or

plants, indigenous or introduced from abroad, which is hardly worth reproducing. He states that halla (hala) pineapple is "not plentiful." What would Macrae say if he returned to the islands in 1922? He would find square miles of pineapples.)

July 19-23. Fine fresh breezes from E.N.E.

July 27. Fine. Breezes E. by S. Crossed the Equator.

DISCOVERY OF MALDEN ISLAND

July 30. Sighted land, at 12 noon. Lowered two boats and landed through the surf on a fine sandy coral beach covered with shells, most of which were the cockle kind of very large size weighing over 15 lbs. We separated to explore the island, and found it low and flat, covered with vegetation of no great variety, being mostly sidas and a few bushes of tournefortia. The island was covered with birds, remarkably tame and easily taken in our hands.

We saw remains of huts built of coral slabs without any timber, and we gathered therefrom that the island had been inhabited, probably by shipwrecked people and never discovered. At one of these huts, the surveyor left a sealed bottle which he had brought for the purpose, containing some written inscription, what, I know not. I saw no signs of cultivation. There was a little fresh water in holes among the coral rocks, a good distance from the sea. Just when our stay was becoming most interesting, the recall gun from the ship was fired, so we could not find out any more about the island. We thought that we might perhaps find something concerning the unfortunate Mr. de la Perouse and his crew, about whom the world still remains doubtful as to what part of these seas they were lost.

This little island, which is a discovery of the Blonde, and since named Malden Island, in honour of our surveyor, is about 12 miles in circumference, is very low and scarcely seen 15 miles distant out at sea. It abounds with sea birds, but without quadrupeds except a small brown shiny kind of short-tailed rat, very wild, that ran into their holes at our approach.

HERE ENDS JAMES MACRAE'S DIARY

The following is a condensed log of H.M.S. Blonde after leaving Malden Island:

1825—Aug.　1—Passed Starbuck Island.
　　　”　　　8—Reached and landed at Mauke, one of the Cook group.
　　Sept.　4—Passed Juan Fernandez.
　　　”　　6—Reached Valparaiso.
　　　”　　29—Anchored at Talcahuana (Concepcion).
　　Oct.　12—Sailed from Concepcion and reached Valparaiso 13th.
　　Dec.　5—At Coquimbo.
　　　”　　29—Doubled Cape Horn.
1826—Jan.　23—Arrived at St. Helena and stayed there until 28th January.
　　Mar.　7—Rescued the survivors of the wrecked ship Frances Mary, bound from New Brunswick for Liverpool.
　　　”　　15—Anchored at Spithead after an absence of seventeen months and fifteen days.